THAI GARDEN STYLE

THAI GARDEN STYLE

Photography by
LUCA INVERNIZZI TETTONI

Text by
WILLIAM WARREN

PERIPLUS
EDITIONS

Published by **Periplus Editions (HK) Ltd**
Copyright © 1996 Periplus Editions (HK) Ltd
ALL RIGHTS RESERVED
Printed in the Republic of Singapore
ISBN 962-593-137-6

Address all enquiries and comments to:
Periplus (Singapore) Pte Ltd,
5 Little Road #08-01, Singapore 536983

Publisher: Eric Oey
Editor: Kim Inglis
Production: Mary Chia, Su T C

ACKNOWLEDGMENTS

A book like this could not be produced without the assistance of many people. The author and photographer are deeply grateful to all those who kindly allowed their private gardens to be photographed, assisted in making countless arrangements and helped with the identification of plant specimens.

We would like to particularly thank Mrs Elisabeth Eber Chan for undertaking the chore of checking plant names and to note that any mistakes that may still be present are our responsibility rather than hers.

We would also like to express our gratitude to Mr Bill Bensley of the Bensley Design Group, Khun Chaiwut Tulayadhan, Khun Chare Chutharatkul, Mr Mark Collins, the management of the Dusit Rayavadee Resort, Mr Skip Heinecke of Royal Garden Resorts, Mr Simon Hirst of the Regent Resort, Khun Jirachai Rengthong of the Bensley Design Group, Khun Lanfaa Devahastin Na Ayudhya, Mr Rusty London, Mr Robert McCarthy, Khun Naphalai Areesorn of Chiva-Som International Health Resorts Co Ltd, Acharn Nitthi Sthapitanond, Khun Patrapara Charusorn, Khun Prabhadibhaya Vadanyakul, Khun Phabhakorn Vadanyakul, Khun Prakong Nucharoen of the Royal Garden Village, Mr Reimund Reisinger, Mr Brian Sherman, Khun Sittichai and Khun Tida Tanpitat, Khun Sirichan Phirompakdi, Khun Suchin and Khun Rujiraporn Wanglee, M L Sudavadee Kriangkrai, Khun Sunanta Tulayadhan, Khun Surasak Hutasewee, Khun Tanu and Inga Malakul, M L Tri Devakul, Khun Tongkham Lakthan, Mr Ed Tuttle, Khun Marisa Viravaidya and Mr Douglas Clayton, Mr Yvan and Khun Wongvipa Van Outrive, and Mr and Mrs Dieter Von Boehm.

Previous page: *A Water Lily pond at the Royal Garden Village at Hua Hin.*

Right: *Terrace of a private villa at the Amanpuri resort, Phuket.*

CONTENTS

PART I   8   *Introduction*
               A general introduction to the history of
               gardens in Thailand

PART II   22   *Bangkok and Environs*

          26   THE JIM THOMPSON GARDEN

          38   THE REGENT HOTEL: INTERIOR
               GARDENING

          44   BAAN SOI KLANG

          50   A PALM LOVER'S GARDEN

PART III 58   *Southern Thailand*

          64   A GARDEN OF UNDERSTATEMENT

          70   THE RAILWAY HOTEL GARDEN

          74   A LANDMARK SEASIDE GARDEN

          84   GARDENING WITH NATURE

          90   A GARDEN ON THE ANDAMAN SEA

PART IV   102   *Northern Thailand*

           112   GARDENS FOR ESCAPE

           124   A NORTHERN RESORT

           128   A GARDEN OF HELICONIAS

           138   A RUSTIC RETREAT

           142   A COLLECTOR'S GARDEN

           148   TWO NORTHERN HOLIDAY GARDENS

           154   A VALLEY GARDEN

           162   A GARDEN BY A MOUNTAIN STREAM

PART V   170   *Gardening in Thailand: A Personal
                  View*
                  *Some observations about the author's
                  experiences as a landscape gardener in Thailand*

           178   *Ideas for Small Gardens*

           189   *Bibliography*

           190   *Index*

INTRODUCTION

"This country is very fertile and, without needing great labour for its cultivation, anything that one may plant flourishes."

Though some contemporary gardeners might question the lack of effort required, most would agree with Jesuit priest Nicholas Gervaise's 17th-century impression of Thailand's exceptional fertility. Its conditions vary widely, ranging from the cool northern highlands to the steamy jungles of the far south, but nearly all are conducive to rapid plant growth that comes as a revelation to anyone more accustomed to the seasonal pace of temperate countries. To early visitors, this was most evident in the rice fields, orchards, vegetable gardens and other clear signs of agricultural abundance which they saw throughout their travels.

Less well documented — indeed, hardly documented at all — are the uses made of this natural wealth for ornamental purposes. Granted, with certain reservations, that "anything that

Opposite: *A stupa rises beside a lake with Water Lilies at Sukothai, the first capital of Thailand.*

one may plant flourishes", what sort of non-commercial gardens were created in traditional Thailand? What specific trees and shrubs were used, how were they arranged, and was there anything distinctively Thai about such arrangements?

The answers to these questions, especially the last one, are not easy. Details in mural paintings provide some information, as do the accounts of visitors like Gervaise. Few written Thai records, however, survived the devastating destruction of Ayutthaya, the old capital, in 1767; and by the time photography arrived, in the mid-19th century, Western and other influences had already begun to change both the concepts and the components of landscape design, along with so much else.

Eighteenth-century Europeans who saw Ayutthaya at its peak of power provide detailed descriptions of the city's architectural splendours and also of such exotic commercial plants as the Betel Nut palm, the Durian and the Mango. They are curiously reticent, though, about the gardens they must have passed through in the royal palace on their way to audiences with King Narai, and the scant information they offer about ornamental plants is both dubious and contradictory. Gervaise, for instance,

Opposite and above: *Two details from Thai murals showing traditional palace gardens. The one on left is from a painted wooden panel. Mango trees—fruiting and flowering—are depicted, with the fruits protected by bamboo baskets until ready to eat, as they still are in many gardens today. A more formal arrangement is shown in the one at Wat Mongkut in Bangkok (above). Here, a Lotus pond, surrounded by flowering trees and shrubs, acts as a focal point. In the upper left are some Toddy palms, which are still widely planted in Thailand.*

of Buddhist monasteries, of royal palaces, and those found around the homes of ordinary people. The plant materials used might overlap to some degree, but the purpose of each differed greatly.

"The numerous courts of the temple open one out of another," wrote an English painter named P A Thompson, describing a Bangkok monastery in the early years of this century. "In some are the rows of small buildings where the monks dwell, each in his own room. Others are filled with leafy trees and artificial rocks and ponds...". Monastery gardens were conceived as places to promote contemplation and peace of mind, achieved through planting mini-forests of often tall trees in courtyards or in the monks' residential section. Many of these were native flowering trees like Saraca, which has orange blossoms, while others could be used in traditional medicine; following its early introduction from the New World tropics some time in the 16th or 17th centuries, the Plumeria became a common monastery tree, as its fragrant, five-petaled flowers were popular as offerings.

Some temple-garden components were included because of their special significance in Buddhism. Thus most large

claims that he saw "roses and carnations, and at all times tuberoses, the scent of which is sweeter than that of ours"; he also mentions Jasmine (both "double and single varieties"), something that is apparently a Gardenia, and "white, red, yellow, and variegated daisies". On the other hand, another early visitor who headed a French embassy to Ayutthaya in 1687 called Simon de la Loubère noted the Tuberoses but says he saw "no roses". He also makes no mention of either Daisies or Carnations (which, even today, are successfully grown only in

the far north) and Jasmine he wrote was "so rare that 'tis said there are none but at the King's House". Fairly, but not very helpfully to anyone trying to reconstruct these ancient gardens, he observes that while there might be a lack of familiar European ornamentals, "they have others which are peculiar to them, and which are very agreeable for their beauty and odour", without specifying or describing any of them.

In any discussion of old Thai gardens, it is useful to keep in mind that there were three more or less distinct categories: those compounds, then as now, contained at least one *Ficus religiosa*, or Bodhi tree, under which the Buddha attained enlightenment, as well as a pond or water jars devoted to *Nelumbo nucifera*, the sacred Lotus, prized as a symbol of perfection by several religions.

Palace gardens, on the other hand, seem to have drawn most of their visual inspiration from Chinese models, perhaps through reports brought back by travellers, or maybe through ancestral memory and tradition. The qualification "seem" is advisable, since except for idealized depictions in old mural paintings, none of the gardens remain. The closest modern equivalent, in Bangkok's Grand Palace compound, has been re-landscaped countless times since its inception, and perhaps the only contemporary features that would be recognizable to the original builders are the trees trained and clipped into odd shapes, a distinctly Chinese horticultural passion.

These clipped trees are what most Thais turn to when they want to add a touch of "traditional" to contemporary gardens. The art of making them is called *mai dat*. In the 1920s Prince Damrong Rachanuphab, known as the Father of Thai History, noted that it was practised in the 13th and 14th centuries in Sukhothai, the country's first

Opposite: A 17th-century temple at Petchaburi, south of Bangkok: The main building is surrounded by pots containing traditional clipped trees, or mai dat, while in the front is an old Plumeria, a flowering tree found in most temple gardens.

Right: Plumerias like the one seen near this group of religious monuments at Wat Raj Bophit in Bangkok were introduced to Southeast Asia from the New World tropics, probably by the Portuguese, but quickly adapted to local conditions.

Below: Ficus religiosa, the Bodhi tree, under which the Buddha attained enlightenment, is regarded as sacred and therefore forbidden to other gardens. The tree can be seen in nearly every temple compound, often wrapped with a cloth to signify its holiness. The one shown here is at Bangkok's Wat Po.

Below: *A classic central-style Thai house. The art of clipping plants like the shrub on the right is known as* mai dat*; inspired by the Chinese, it is believed to date from the first Thai capital of Sukhothai.*

Opposite: *A clipped tree at Bangkok's Grand Palace, perhaps the most authentic example of a classic Thai garden, originally built toward the end of the 18th century. A number of plants are trained in this way, the one here being* Diospyros rhodocalyx, *popularly known as the Siamese Rough Bush.*

independent capital. A number of different plants are used, both trees and shrubs, the most common being *Diospyros rhodocalyx* (*tako* in Thai), which has small, rough leaves; *Streblus asper* (*khoi*), the leaves of which are also used for making paper; Tamarind (*ma-kham*); and *Wrightia religiosa* (*mok*), a shrub with scented flowers.

Nine popular *mai dat* designs evolved during the Ayutthaya period, each usually consisting of an odd number of clipped leaf formations on branches emerging from the trunk. Though the results are often displayed in decorative pots like a Japanese bonsai, the two art forms are very different; whereas the bonsai (always potted) is a miniature tree that aims to replicate the original in shape, the *mai dat*, in a pot or as part of a landscape, is angular and abstract, and like traditional Thai floral arrangements amounts to a re-creation rather than an imitation of nature.

Another traditional feature—also of probable Chinese inspiration—that can still be seen in some gardens is the *khao mor*, an artificial mountain made of pebbles or larger stones cemented together to form a whole, often with waterfalls and pools and adorned with *mai dat* or ordinary plants. These may be miniature versions in shallow

pots or sizeable creations incorporated into the garden design; a large one in the inner part of the Grand Palace was the site of several important ceremonies such as the cutting of the top-knot when children reached puberty.

As in China, Thai palaces consisted of various enclosed sections, each serving a particular function. The outer areas were relatively bare of greenery, often paved with cobblestones and devoted to government offices and audience halls; the real gardens lay behind high walls, designed for the private pleasure of the King, his wives, and their attendants (which is perhaps why the French visitors quoted earlier never saw them).

No record remains of the gardens in the royal palace of Ayutthaya, but they were probably similar to the early ones in the Bangkok palace which was in many respects deliberate replica. Here the original plants are said to have included varieties chosen because of their fragrance, among them *Michelia champaca alba* (*champi* in Thai), a member of the Magnolia family; Jasmine (*mali-sorn*); *Mimusops elengi* (*pikul*), the flowers of which were used to scent clothes and make potpourri; and *Mammea siamensis* (*sarapee*), an evergreen tree with white blooms. There were numerous ponds, planted with Water Lilies and Lotus, as well as *khao mors* to create an illusion of topography in an otherwise flat landscape. An illustration in a travel account by the Marquis of Beauvoir, who was received by King Mongkut in Bangkok in 1867, is captioned "Un arroyo à Bangkok" but is almost certainly taken from a photograph of one of the pools in the Grand Palace garden; among the prominent plants is what appears to be a wild Dracaena (*chandhana*), which produces sprays of fragrant flowers.

Prince Chula Chakrabongse notes in his history of the Chakri Dynasty that, in the early 19th century, King Rama II redesigned the original garden that had been planted by his father. He created one with a large lake, lined with bricks, which had several islands, large and small, all connected together by charming little bridges of diverse designs. On some of the islands there were Chinese pagodas, on others little European pavilions, and the King took his meals or listened to music in these delightful buildings. There was boating on the lake, and sometimes evening parties were held when the Court went into fancy dress, and all the little canoes which were paddled around the islands had bright lamps of myriad hues." The description is strikingly similar to many written about the Imperial Palace in Beijing.

"Khun Chang Khun Pan", the narrative poem written by Thai poet Sunthorn Phu in the early 19th century, contains an episode in which Khun Pan slips into the house of his love, Nang Pim. The author lists various potted plants on her verandah, which were no doubt typical of those to be seen in both palaces and aristocratic households of the time, among them *Michelia champaca alba*, a Dwarf Tamarind tree with its branches clipped into balls, *Pandanus odoratissimus* (*lumchiek*), *Jasminium sambac* (*mali-sorn*), *Melodorum fruticosum* (*lamduan*) and *Sansevieria trifasciata* (*ked*).

Aesthetic considerations were secondary in the gardens of most ordinary homes. Here the emphasis was on practicality—plants that could be used for food,

Above: *An engraving of a pool in the Grand Palace garden in the mid-19th century, taken from a photograph and entitled "Un arroyo à Bangkok". The tall, palm-like plants are a wild Dracaena with fragrant flowers. This pool, part of a large artificial mountain, was used in a variety of royal ceremonies.*

Opposite top: *Clipped mai dat specimens in the Wat Po enclosure.*

Opposite left: *An artificial mountain: such creations, called khao mor, were popular features in traditional Thai palace and temple gardens and ranged in size from small to quite large.*

such as fruit trees, and a vast variety of culinary herbs, and others that yielded the ingredients for traditional medicines. The arrangement, more often than not, was haphazard, with little attention given to present-day concepts of landscape design.

Superstition played (and to some extent continues to play) a significant role. A Star Gooseberry (*Phyllanthus acidus*; in Thai *ma-yom*) is regarded as lucky when planted at the front of a house since its Thai name sounds like the word for "popularity". Almost any plant whose Thai name begins with the syllable *ma* is, in fact, considered auspicious: *ma-krut* (Kaffir Lime), *ma-muang* (Mango), *ma-fuang* (Starfruit), *ma-kham* (Tamarind) and *ma-la-kaw* (Papaya). The fact that they also produce fruit is perhaps not entirely coincidental. Other plants, however, without any practical use, are also looked upon as auspicious and often grown as much-prized potted specimens. Many of these are notable for their patterned leaves, like Codiaeum, Caladium, Dieffenbachia and Aglaonema, as well as almost anything with gold-coloured foliage.

Other plants were considered to be unlucky, at least in non-royal, non-religious compounds. Plumeria was one, since its Thai name, *lan-tom*, is similar to *ran-tom*,

Below: *Khao Wang, "the Mountain Palace", built by King Rama IV in the mid-19th century atop a hill in Petchaburi and recently restored by the Fine Arts Department; the compounds include an observation tower for astronomical studies, the King's favourite pastime. Rarely seen in private gardens, Plumerias were often seen in royal and religious gardens.*

Opposite top: *A building in Khao Wang, showing one of the numerous old Plumeria trees which were planted along the road leading up to the palace.*

Opposite bottom: *Colonade at the hilltop palace in Petchaburi; pots of Bougainvillea line the wall and, behind them, some of the original Plumeria trees, now more than a century old.*

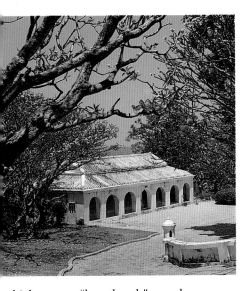

which means "heartbreak"; another was a kind of fern called *prong*, since that sounds like *plong*, meaning "to dispose of". M R Pimsai Amranand, an authority on Thai gardening, also lists others. She says that *Bombax ceiba* (*ngiu*), a native tree with red-orange flowers, was excluded because its soft wood is used in making coffins; Hibiscus because condemned criminals were once paraded through the streets with a red Hisbiscus flower behind their ears; and *Clerodendrum fragrans* (*nang yaem*) because older plants were supposed to turn into spirits. Modern gardeners appear to have overcome most of these prejudices, though many still refuse to include Plumerias in their landscape plan.

M R Pimsai developed her love of gardening in England where she lived for much of her younger life, and was frankly horrified by most of the Thai gardens she saw on her return in the 1950s. Her first impression, she later wrote, was "of flat pieces of land with spindly fruit trees planted all along the fences, with herbs and flowers planted in ugly raised beds completely straight, looking vaguely like graves. Or sometimes one would be introduced to someone who was thought to be a great gardener, and on going to his house one would see no garden but a collection of Crotons, Gerbera or orchids, all grown in straight rows or in pots. The emphasis was on the plants, with little thought of how a garden should look. The word *suan* in Thai and translated as 'garden' conjures up in Thai minds a place the English would call an orchard or a market garden."

Soon after that was written the situation was to change dramatically. Such Western concepts of landscape design as lawns and massed beds became common, while to meet the growing demand for horticultural novelty both private collectors and nursery owners introduced countless new ornamental specimens from tropical places as distant as Hawaii and South America. The choice of Heliconias, for example, was limited to only a few varieties as recently as the 1970s; within a decade there were dozens, along with such related species as Alpinia and flowering Bananas. Moreover, Thai commercial growers became expert at developing new hybrids of Codiaeum, Aglaonema, Dieffenbachia, Cordylines and others, often assigning them impressive names to increase their desirability (and, inevitably, their prices).

Thai garden styles today reflect as wide a variety of tastes as can be found anywhere in the tropics. Some show a continuing fondness for the neatly clipped shrubs of old palace arrangements, though the plants used are more likely to be flowering species like Bougainvillea and Lantana than the less colourful traditional ones. Others are what M R Pimsai calls "status gardens": "Their trees are usually slow-growing imported palms or conifers. The flower beds, and beds of roses and annuals, all show only too well the army of gardeners they must have to keep the places in such

perfect condition." Another characteristic of such landscapes is a penchant for abstract designs largely created by beds of plants with coloured foliage, requiring constant maintenance for its effect. In the cooler north, one sees gardens that in both design and plant materials are scarcely distinguishable from those in an English village.

Increasingly, however, more imaginative designers are emphasizing the country's tropical luxuriance, creating mini-jungles that blend native and imported plants in an artfully natural way. In doing so, they have been responsible for some of the finest of tropical gardens—not, perhaps, specifically "Thai", but nonetheless making full use of the country's fabled fertility.

Top left: Jasminum rex, *a climber with unscented flowers.*

Top right: Artabotrys hexapetalus, *strongly scented at night.*

Middle left: Cananga odorata, *the flowers of which are used to scent cloth.*

Middle right: *A cultivar of* Plumeria rubra—*the flowers may be many different colours.*

Far left: Phyllanthus acidus, *the Star Gooseberry, traditionally planted near the gate of a house.*

Left: Michelia champaca alba, *the very fragrant white-flowering Champaca.*

Opposite: Cassia fistula, *popularly known as the Golden Shower tree or the Indian Laburnum and designated as Thailand's national tree. Its cascades of bright yellow are a prominent feature of Thai gardens and roadways during the hot season.*

BANGKOK AND ENVIRONS

Bangkok is situated on the banks of the Chao Phraya River in the lower part of the flat, alluvial Central Plains, one of the world's richest rice-growing regions. Prior to becoming the seat of government in 1782, it was a prosperous little trading port surrounded by plantations of Coconut and Betel Nut palms, where ships called en route to the splendid former capital of Ayutthaya further up-river. Later, like Ayutthaya, it became known to Western visitors as the Venice of the East, due to the network of canals that served as its streets. These, as the city prospered, increasingly led further and further away from the original centre containing the mile-square Grand Palace.

Even though the first roads appeared in the mid-19th century, the city remained essentially water-oriented until World War II. Most commercial and residential properties were close to either the river or one of the canals, even though motor vehicles had already replaced boats as the preferred form of transportation for most residents.

Opposite: *Tall Livistona fan palms and clambering creepers help create a tropical atmosphere in the Bangkok garden of Jim Thompson's house. The house and garden are now open to the public.*

Below: *A small garden in Bangkok, with a Thai-style lamp and rustic deck chair.*

Opposite: *A modern reproduction of a Ghandara sculpture surveys the scene from a balcony outside the living room of Bill Bensley's Thai-style house; trees and palms outside as well as potted plants provide a sense of tropical luxuriance.*

The change began in the early 1950s and accelerated with remarkable speed. Leaving the river, the general population moved in other directions, first eastward toward the Gulf of Thailand and later northward into the Central Plains, bringing housing estates and new business centres to what were rice fields within the memory of middle-aged residents. Today the city covers a vast area on both sides of the Chao Phraya, its population estimated at close to 10 million, and most of the old canals have been filled in to make way for yet more urgently-needed roads.

All these factors—be they geographical, historical and social—are relevant to contemporary urban gardeners. Most of the city lies almost at sea level and, due to indiscriminate pumping of underground water, some of it is a metre or more below. This means that many parts are subject to floods, especially the eastern suburbs, an area which two centuries ago was known as the Sea of Mud and was regarded as a natural deterrent to any invader approaching from that direction. Nor is the northern sprawl much safer; a combination of high tides and heavy rainfall up-country left thousands of gardens and fruit orchards under water for months in 1995.

The heavy clay soil so hospitable to rice growing is less well suited to the cultivation of more delicate ornamentals, thus requiring a considerable amount of preparation before a really healthy garden can be established. Finally, the present population density and the rapid increase of high-rise construction have almost eliminated the spacious gardens of the past, along with many of the larger trees that gave them their character.

Yet Bangkok remains the gardening centre of Thailand, just as it remains the cultural and commercial heart. The best plant nurseries are located there, constantly introducing new species, along with the best landscape designers and the greatest number of people with money to employ their skills. Less affluent residents, too, take a greater interest in horticulture than those in other regions, even when forced to work in severely restricted spaces.

From the vantage point of a traffic-clogged street, the prospects may seem unpromising. But hidden behind the high walls characteristic of most residential areas, awaiting discovery along the well-guarded streets of suburban estates, are plantings of exceptional beauty that still set the ultimate standards for Thai gardens.

THE JIM THOMPSON GARDEN

Above: *An old bench in the garden of the Jim Thompson house; the cushions are covered with the silk he made world-famous.*

Opposite: *A jungle-like atmosphere is created in the garden through such plants as Spathiphyllum, Cordyline and Rhapis palms, all of which flourish in filtered sunlight.*

Jim Thompson, an American who came to Thailand in 1945, became internationally famous for a variety of achievements—his revival of the Thai silk industry, the comprehensive collection of Asian art he assembled, and the beautiful Thai-style home he built on a Bangkok klong. Less well known except to his close friends was his enthusiasm for tropical gardening, which began in the small compound of his first house and continued in the more spacious area around the Thai structures into which he moved in 1959. A large Rain tree (*Samanea saman*) already grew on the site and provided shade for the terrace overlooking the klong, and Thompson added a number of Flame trees (*Delonix regia*) as well as a jungle-like planting of shrubs and creepers. By the time he disappeared in 1967 in northern Malaysia, the garden was well-established and had become an integral part of the overall atmosphere.

One of the joys of creating a garden in the tropics is the extraordinary speed of growth. Without regular attention, however, this apparent blessing can become a threat and

Above: The terrace of the Thompson house, which architecturally is the front and overlooks a canal; the large Rain tree that shades the area was already growing on the site when the house was built in 1959. In the foreground, left, are Codiaeum and yellow Ixora.

Left: Steps leading to the front terrace, planted with Alpinia, Cordylines, palms and foliage Heliconias.

Opposite: The guest wing of the Thompson house overlooks a luxuriant garden of palms and flowering shrubs. On the left is a Ficus elastica commonly called the Rubber plant which has been topped to create a bushier appearance.

Overleaf: Among the plants to be seen from the open area beneath the house are Dieffenbachia with green and white patterned leaves, Alocasia (Elephant's Ear) and Alpinia purpurata (Red Ginger); in the background is a stand of Golden Bamboo.

eventually a serious problem. Such was the fate that befell the Thompson garden. Wild Ficus trees took root and eventually crowded out less robust specimens, while other, originally more decorative trees and palms grew into giants that blocked necessary sunlight from reaching flowering shrubs; twenty-five years after Jim Thompson disappeared, the house—now a public museum—was almost hidden by a haphazard tangle of growth and the garden had lost much of its original distinction.

A major restoration took place in 1994-95 involving a number of locally-based landscape designers, among them the Bensley Design Group and Reimund Reisinger. The wild Ficus were removed, along with their invasive roots, a task that left the main garden virtually bare except for a few palms and smaller trees. New laterite pathways were then laid in this area, older ones in areas along the klong were reconstructed to create raised beds, and large quantities of fresh soil and fertilizer were brought in to enrich the entire garden.

Around the terrace, over which the Rain tree still spreads its branches, raised beds have been replanted with a variety of foliage specimens that include Codiaeum, Cordyline, Aglaonema, variegated Alpinia,

Below: *The ornamental leaves on the left are* Heliconia indica, *while the variegated ground cover is* Acorus gramineus.

Opposite: *Along a laterite pathway lined with Ophiopogon grow red Ixora, green and yellow variegated Alpinia and, behind the water jar, a stand of Golden Bamboo. In the background can be seen the staff quarters, also in Thai style.*

Dieffenbachia, self-heading Philodendron (*P. bipinartifidum*) and Calathea, while a fence added for security reasons along the canal has been covered with *Thunbergia grandiflora*, a fast-growing vine, as well as a screen of fragrant *Murraya paniculata* (Mock Orange).

New laterite pathways have been laid in the main garden, where the sunlight that now streams through the remaining trees has facilitated the growth of many more blooming shrubs. Among those used prominently are Hibiscus, Ixora, Heliconia, Caesalpinia (the Peacock Flower), *Alpinia purpurata* (Red Ginger), *Duranta repens* (Golden Dewdrop) and flowering Bananas. In areas with more filtered light, Scindapsus and Spathiphyllum are used as ground covers, with colourful accents provided by Codiaeum, Cordyline and a variegated Crinum. A jungle-like effect is produced by Alocasias (Elephant's Ears) and ornamental palms. Throughout the garden are displayed old water jars and sculpture from Thomson's large collection.

Once again the Jim Thompson garden complements the elegant lines of the old Thai structures he put together with such discerning taste and left as a memorial to an extraordinary career.

Above: *Spathiphyllum (front left) and Dieffenbachia with white leaves (right) bring variety to this predominantly shady part of the Thompson garden; in the background is an antique water jar.*

Right: *A pond lined with laterite in the centre of the garden: Low-growing Cuphea softens the edge in the foreground, while other plants include Red Ginger (Alpinia purpurata), variegated Alpinia zerumbet, Pandanus amaryllifolius, Crinum Lilies and red Ixora.*

Opposite top: *A laterite pathway leads through densely-planted beds of Dieffenbachia, Spathiphyllum, Cordylines and self-heading Philodendron.*

Left: Tall palms and flowering Bananas rise above the mass of tropical greenery in the Thompson garden, which now looks much as it did when the owner lived there.

Below: The luxuriance of fan palms can be seen through the windows of the elegant panelled teak drawing room; a Khmer-style head stands on top of a cabinet with gold and black lacquer paintings on the right.

THE REGENT HOTEL: INTERIOR GARDENING

Above: *A large* Philodendron bipinartifidum *hangs over a pool of bright carp.*

Opposite: *A pool linking the hotel lobby with the ballroom is planted with purple-flowering* Thalia geniculata *(Water Canna) and* Cyperus alternifolius *(Umbrella Plant), with* Aglaonema *and ferns in the foreground.*

Except for narrow strips along the front and sides, Bangkok's low-rise Regent Hotel occupies almost all the building site. It nevertheless manages to provide a sense of tropical luxuriance through the use of two dramatic atriums, one large and the other small, which were part of the original design, as well as an open garden area added later as a link to the hotel ballroom. Sitthiporn Dhonavan, who was responsible for planting the larger atrium, is one of Thailand's pioneering designers of contemporary gardens, favouring a lush, natural effect over the more traditional clipped, formal arrangements. Over the course of his long career, he has also been a notable plant collector and has not only introduced countless new ornamental specimens from distant places but also hybridized many others.

For the Regent's Parichart Court, open to the sky and therefore spared the difficulties imposed by air-conditioning and lack of natural light and rain, he created an evocative mini-

Left and far left: *Dieffenbachia and Aglaonema cultivars, both shade-loving plants, are noted for their leaf patterns. They are popular as house plants due to their ability to survive indoors for long periods.*

Below: *Prominent features of the Parichart Court garden are a variegated Pandanus veitchii, a Prichardia fan palm, and Philodenron bipinartifidum. Spathiphyllum and Rhoeo are used as ground covers.*

Above: *Outside one of the restaurants, a waterfall is planted with* Cyperus alternifolius, Dieffenbachia, Maranta *and ferns. A locally-made ceramic frog adds a whimsical touch.*

jungle with a small waterfall that cascades over boulders and eventually flows into a tranquil pool in which swim colourful carp. Ficus trees, Fishtail palms (*Caryota mitis*), tufted Chrysalidocarpus palms and feathery stands of Bamboo provide height in the landscape, while other specimens include variegated Pandanus, *Dracaena fragrans*, Red Ginger, Rhapis palms, *Philodendron bipinartifidum* and Livistona palms with enormous fan-shaped leaves. Lower growing plants include Spathiphyllum, Aglaonema, Dieffenbachia, Scindapsis and ferns. The garden effect is continued on the floors overlooking the atrium through containers planted with Heliconias and Bougainvillea.

Following renovations a few years ago, the small atrium in the Monthathip Court was redesigned by Pusadee Muntabhorn in a sparser style, with a ground covering of smooth river pebbles, a fish pool, and carefully spaced Ficus trees, Rhapis palms *Philodendron bipinartifidum* and *Wrightia religiosa* with small white fragrant flowers.

Khun Pusadee, who received her design training in the United States, was also given the job of planting a new 180-square-metre garden outside the ballroom and one of the hotel restaurants. Divided into two sections on either side of a walkway, this receives a considerable amount of sunlight, which allows the use of a number of flowering specimens. The two areas are linked by a pool and both are densely planted with tall Ficus, yellow-blooming *Cassia surattensis*, *Wrightia religiosa*, *Melia azedarach* (Persian Lilac), *Callistemon lanceolatus* (Bottlebrush), Rhapis palms and, hanging over the water, *Philodendron bipinartifidum*.

Left: *A variegated Crinum Lily adds an interesting touch of white to the predominantly green atrium garden; the ground cover is Syngonium.*

Opposite: *Pandanus veitchii arches over a water feature in the Parichart Court; on the left are Spathiphyllum.*

Above: *Large stands of Etlingera elatior, the Torch Ginger, rise on either side of the main entrance stair; other plants in the arrangement include Dieffenbachia,* Philodendron bipinartifidum *and Dracaena fragrans.*

Opposite: *The plant-filled living room, reflected in the swimming pool by night, makes for a dramatic setting.*

BAAN SOI KLANG

Soi Klang, off Bangkok's Sukhumwit Road, was once a quiet residential street of houses set in large, shady gardens. This atmosphere is rapidly changing as high-rise condominiums go up along much of its length and many compounds are converted for commercial use. As a result, many former residents have moved to the suburbs, but one family still enjoys the old sense of spacious privacy, enhanced by a luxuriant and in some ways unusual garden.

Baan Soi Klang, as the house is called, is hidden from the street by a dense planting of trees and shrubs along a sloping drive that leads up to a courtyard. In most other Bangkok landscapes of comparable scale, at least a few of these trees would be fruit-bearing, probably Mangoes, or else they would be expensive specimens that proclaim the prosperity of the owner. Here, though, the trees planted are either relatively common or native species. Among the latter is *Barringtonia asiatica*, a handsome tree with glossy dark-green leaves more usually seen in seaside gardens; the owner brought back seeds from a visit to the far south

Below: *The terrace and an atrium are transformed into an interior garden through the use of such potted specimens as Alocasia (Elephant's Ear), Philodendron and various Dieffenbachia cultivars.*

Right: *Asplenium nidus (Bird's Nest fern) and Aglaonema* pictum *provide a setting for this stone garden figure.*

Far right: *A sunny terrace beside the pool is the perfect spot for al fresco dining; in the background are palms and Ficus trees.*

Above: A massed display of shade-tolerant potted plants brings green to the curved window of the living room. The owner periodically changes this arrangement depending on the effect desired. The floor of the container is covered with smooth river pebbles for a natural look.

and found it grew just as well under the very different conditions of Bangkok. Another is *Butea monosperma*, popularly called the Flame of the Forest, which grows wild in various parts of Thailand and has bright vermillion flowers. Several Royal palms (*Roystonea regia*), *Brassaia actinophylla* (the Octopus tree) and large Ficus trees also serve as screens.

Clipped Bougainvilleas, *Streblus asper*, and *Malpighia coccigera* lend a formal touch to the planting near the entrance, though

this is relieved by a stand of Torch Ginger (*Etlingera elatoir*) and the large, dramatic leaves of *Philodendron bipinartifidum*.

The house consists of two main sections connected by a terrace around and over a swimming pool. The main living room overlooks an atrium filled with large potted plants—among them Rhapis palms, Brassaia, Dieffenbachia and assorted Philodendrons—and most areas have soothing views of the pool and a large garden at the rear of the property. Trees in this section include *Ficus benjamina*, Plumeria, *Ficus elastica*, *Michelia champaca alba*, *Pisonia alba* and more *Barringtonia asiatica*. There are some Heliconias and Hibiscus, but on the whole flowering plants are used sparsely, colour being provided by such foliage specimens as Maranta, Calathea, Dieffenbachia and Cordyline.

Stepping stones lead down to a lower area of the back garden where there is a pond for water lilies, surrounded by beds of Spathiphyllums, variegated Pandanus and stands of Bamboo and Phoenix palms.

Amid the changes around it, Baan Soi Klang stands as a restful green oasis in central Bangkok and also serves as an example of what other city gardeners could achieve with the proper dedication.

Below: *Artfully placed stepping stones lead through the main lawn; the tree in the background is a* Ficus, *while the low variegated plant on the left is* Dianella ensifolia.

Opposite: *A Water Lily pond in a corner of the garden adds a cool note. The tall plants are* Typha angustifolia, *while the variegated leaves in the background are* Pandanus veitchii.

A PALM LOVER'S GARDEN

Palms are virtually an emblem of the tropics, and it is a rare Thai garden that does not contain at least a few of them, mostly Coconuts or tufted palms like *Ptychosperma macarthurii*, which grow rapidly with little effort. Serious Palmae collectors, however, are relatively rare, partly because of the slow-growing nature of some, more, perhaps, because of the high prices commanded by rarer specimens imported from abroad. One of the most notable collections is to be seen in a large garden designed by Surasak Hutasewee in the Rangsit District just north of Bangkok.

The garden's theme is apparent in a dense mass of varied palms planted along the street outside the compound, their fronds almost concealing the wall, and it is continued along two sides of the parking area within the gate. Here and in the main garden behind the house are planted 60-odd different palm varieties, ranging from the comparatively common—used mostly for screening purposes—to the exotic and unfamiliar.

Particularly striking is *Copernicia macroglossa*, popularly called the "Cuban Petticoat Palm" because of the dead leaves that tend to hang below its tightly folded cluster of huge green leaves. *C. baileyana*, also native to Cuba, is a taller fan palm that grows up to 15 metres tall, with a thick trunk and leathery leaves in a dense crown. Several varieties of Livistona are incorporated into the landscape, among them *L. decipiens*, known in its native Australia as "Weeping Cabbage", which has fan-shaped leaves that droop picturesquely at the tips, and the smaller *L. muelleri*, the Dwarf fan palm, which comes from northeastern Australia and New Guinea. *Bismarckia nobilis*, originally from Madagascar, is a majestic species with grey-green leaves that can measure several metres across, while *Corypha elata* is a large handsome

Left: The garden's palm theme is announced just inside the entrance gate, where half a dozen different varieties including Sabal, Livistona, Wodyetia 'foxtail', Rhopaloblaste, Acoelorrhaphe wrightii 'silver saw' and Pritchardia are planted along the parking area. Orchids climb up the trunk of the Rhopaloblaste on the right. The blooming plants in the left foreground are Euphorbias, which are considered to bring the owner good fortune.

Far left: Cycas circinalis, *a non-flowering plant that is often mistaken for a palm, but is not of the Palmae family. Dramatic plants for a tropical garden, cycads are amongst the oldest plants in the world, once providing food for dinosaurs.*

Left: Dasylirion glaucophyllum, *rarely seen in Thai gardens.*

Below: *On the right is* Zamia furfuracea *which makes a striking focal point in a garden. On the left is a* Dasylirion.

…an-palm native to Southeast Asia which …dies after producing a spectacular six-…netre inflorescence above its crown. One …of the oddest specimens in the collection is …he famous Double Coconut (*Lodoicea mal-…ivica*) from the Seychelles, also called …"Coco-de-Mer" since its double-lobed nuts …ften float in the sea for many months …oefore taking root on a distant shore; and …one of the rarest and most beautiful is …*Kerriodoxa elegans*, a native of southern …Thailand with leaves that are glossy green …on top and silvery beneath.

Together with its predominant palms, …which include amongst others *Arecastrum …romanzoffianum*, the "Queen Palm", with a …graceful crown of arching plumelike …fronds, *Butia capita*, the "Jelly Palm", with …edible orange fruit and *Dictyosperma album*, …he "Princess Palm", the garden is home to …members of the Cycadaceae family, that are …among the oldest plants on earth. There are …also several varieties of Heliconia, unusual …Philodendrons and native Thai orchids, …many growing on the palm trunks.

Above right: *Natural stones are used to create a raised bed …in which are planted ground Orchids, Cycads and palms.*

Right: *An unusual Hoya cultivar.*

Far right: *A hybrid Anthurium.*

Left: Orchids, such as this Rhynchostylis gigantea, *hang from trees scattered throughout the garden.*

Below: Bismarckia nobilis: *This large palm which may grow higher than eight metres is originally from Madagascar, where it has almost become extinct.*

Above: Seeds of many palms, such as these pictured here, make interesting decorative additions to any garden.

Above: On the left is the trunk of a Corypha, largest of the fan palms, while on the right is a Hyophorbe vershaffeltii, sometimes known as the Champagne Cork palm due to the shape of its lower trunk.

Right: Scattered amongst the palms are a variety of ground covers. Here, the plant with ferny leaves is a Cycas, while the creeper is a variety of Allamanda with silvery leaves.

Above: *Assorted fan palms line a walkway leading beside the house to the main garden; the owner has collected rare specimens from all over the world, including the large-leafed Borassodendron in the foreground on left.*

Opposite: *Stunning colours and waxy, shining leaves are features of these Bromeliads growing in a moist area near a pool; all these here belong to the Aechmea group. Bromeliads are difficult to grow in Bangkok and therefore not often seen in gardens there.*

Opposite: The blue waters of the Gulf of Thailand lie just beyond the stone walls of the Chiva-Som Health Spa; as is typical of gardens on Thailand's coastline, Coconut palms, the ground cover Wedelia triloba and Crinum Lilies in raised planters above the beach have been chosen because of their ability to withstand salty sea winds.

SOUTHERN THAILAND

The sea is a dominant aspect of Thai life in the regions that lie south and southwest of Bangkok. Nearly 2,000 kilometres of coastlines stretch along the Gulf of Thailand and some 740 along the Indian Ocean and Andaman Sea on the other side of the long, slender peninsula that extends down to Malaysia. The landscape varies from flat, sandy stretches to dramatic limestone cliffs, while the rice fields so typical elsewhere in the country give way to vast plantations of Pineapple, Coconut palms and Rubber trees. Rainfall is sparse in some areas, in others plentiful enough to nurture lush jungles that spill right down to the white sand of idyllic beaches.

Though the natural resources of the South brought prosperity to many of its residents, even those areas fairly close to the capital remained relatively remote until the early years of the present century. In 1911, as part of the entertainment for foreign royalty who attended

the coronation of King Rama VI, Prince Chakrabongse (a young brother of the new king) arranged a tiger hunt for Prince William of Sweden on the western coast of the gulf. An elaborate camp was set up for the party, which also included Prince Chakrabongse's wife. Their son, Prince Chula, later recalled: "My mother was deeply impressed by the beauty of the place. The beach was so wide and the sand was so white and soft as snow. Beyond the plain by the sea there was a range of wooded hills, so that between the hills on one side and the bright blue sea on the other, it was destined to be an ideal seaside resort."

The place was called Hua Hin, and a year or two later Prince Chakrabongse built a bungalow on the beach. When Hua Hin became a stop on the southern railway, other Bangkok aristocrats, including the King, also built seaside retreats—and Thailand's first resort was born. The second was Pattaya, which became popular in the 1950s, followed by more-distant Phuket 20-odd years later. The pattern of development for each was similar: first fairly simple accommodations (except for some of the royal residences at Hua Hin), then hotels, finally holiday homes of a more permanent nature, often with extensive gardens.

Below: *Built on a steep slope overlooking the Andaman Sea, the Phuket Yacht Club was the first luxury hotel to be built in Phuket. Some of the original Coconut palms can be seen against the sky, while the entrance planting includes yellow-leafed Pisonia and pink Mussaenda; trailing from balcony planters is* Wedelia triloba.

Left: *The Yacht Club terraces had to be planted with quick-growing shrubs and ground covers to hold the soil during heavy rains. The one here is planted with Pisonia and Crinum lilies.*

Below: *This dramatic view from the top left of the resort, overlooking Nai Harn Beach, shows Bougainvillea and Allamanda planted in terrace containers. Below are some of the original palm trees on the site.*

Gardening by the sea presents a number of challenges. There is often a shortage of water, especially on islands like Phuket, and the soil tends to be sandy. During the monsoon season, coastal areas of the far south are exposed to strong, salty winds which can have a dire effect on more tender introduced ornamentals unless some sort of screening is provided.

Dedicated gardeners have responded in a variety of ways. Attractive indigenous species well adapted to local conditions—trees like *Barringtonia asiatica* and *Terminalia catappa*, for example, and shrubs like *Scaevola taccada* (Sea Lettuce) and *Pandanus odoratissimus* (Seashore Screwpine)—are incorporated into the landscape design, sometimes even predominating and special areas are created through architecture or judicious planting to accommodate less tolerant specimens. Such efforts have resulted in a number of superb gardens that differ both botanically and in atmosphere from those elsewhere in the country.

Above: *Sunset at Kata Beach. In the foreground are Casuarina, among the commonest of seaside trees.*

Right: *An evening scene at the Sheraton Grande Laguna in Phuket, where Coconut palms display their feathery fronds against a sunset; the distinctive roofs of Thai-style buildings can be seen in the background.*

A Garden of Understatement

Above: *The almost abstract shape of wild Dracaenas blend with the simple lines of this courtyard; between them a terracotta image of a Hindu stands on a base surrounded by water.*

Opposite: *Mounted on clear blocks of plexiglass, these classic water jars seem to float on the surface of a pool at the entrance to the guest wing of the resort; a dense planting of Bamboo, pale-leafed Pisonia, Coconut palms and other trees behind is a reminder of the tropical luxuriance outside.*

The entrance courtyard of Chiva-Som, a health spa at Hua Hin on the Gulf of Thailand, is restrained to the point of austerity: high stone walls and a reception area of elegant simplicity, the only horticultural statement being tall pots of pristine white Bougainvillea. As a guest soon discovers, there is indeed a garden beyond, of unusual beauty, but here, too, the prevailing ambiance is one of understatement rather than of tropical luxuriance.

Plain buildings and pavilions with steep, classic Thai-style roofs are reflected in a large pond below the lobby. Here, many of the plants are white-flowering or have variegated foliage: Tabernaemontana, which resembles a Gardenia but with smaller blooms; variegated Hibiscus; *Wrightia religiosa*, a favourite of old Thai gardens; white Lotus (*Nelumbo nucifera*) in large water jars; *Bauhinia acuminata*, a small tree; Hymenocallis; and beds of Spathiphyllum. Even a group of Mango trees, heavy with fruit, have a neat, orderly appearance. Though colour is certainly present, in the form of Cannas grown in containers in the pond, bright

Above: *Bougainvillea in tall, glazed water jars stand behind a wall covered with Wedelia triloba; the panel with Khmer-style figures on the right is a contemporary reproduction made in northern Thailand.*

Opposite: *Hibiscus with variegated leaves is used as a hedge along the walls of a guest pavilion.*

Below: *The Chiva-Som swimming pool: the smaller Thai-style pavilion is a shelter for guest towels, while the larger one is used for exercises in the morning as the sun rises from the Gulf of Thailand.*

Opposite: *Meticulously clipped shrubs—among them Ixora, Hamelia patens and Murraya paniculata—give a traditional atmosphere to the garden areas surrounding the Thai-style guest pavilions. Along the walkway Wedelia triloba has been clipped to spell out the name of the health spa, an innovative use of this popular ground cover.*

yellow *Pandanus pygmaeus* used as a ground cover, scarlet and purple Bougainvilleas spilling over walls, and a bed of red and white "Lady Di" *Heliconia psittacorum*, it does not predominate.

Another garden area, surrounded by luxurious private guest quarters, consists of a soft, green lawn, dotted with clipped shrubs and trees, among them *Murraya paniculata*, *Duranta repens*, *Malpighia coccigera* (known in Thailand as Singapore Holly), *Hamelia patens* and Ficus trees that have been trained as standards. *Wedelia triloba*, a fast-growing ground cover, is kept severely clipped as well, until it forms a tight carpet along pathways or, in some places, softens the stone walls. There are beds of hanging *Heliconia pendula* and flowering shrubs and such ornamental trees as *Cassia fistula* (the Golden Shower tree), *Delonix regia* (the Flame tree), Tabebuia, Plumeria, Lagerstroemia and *Peltophorum pterocarpum*; again, however, the atmosphere is formal.

Tall Royal palms (*Roystonea regia*) overlook the swimming pool on the beach side, where raised beds exposed to sea winds are planted with hardy *Crinum asiaticum* and trailing *Wedelia tribola*. The setting is truly designed to soothe the soul as well as invigorate the body.

Above: *A topiary elephant shaped from Diospyros rhodocalyx, a large shrub commonly known as Siamese Rough Bush. This tree is often used for these huge creations, regarded as the pride of many traditional Thai gardens.*

Opposite: *Topiary animals and abstract shapes in the garden of the old wing of the hotel, dating from the 1920s; a Bougainvillea hedge blooms in the foreground.*

THE RAILWAY HOTEL GARDEN

Built in 1923, the Railway Hotel in Hua Hin, now called the Sofitel Central, was the grandest of a number erected by the State Railways of Thailand along its southern and northern lines. It also quickly became the most popular since at the time Hua Hin was the only seaside resort easily accessible from Bangkok. The King of Thailand had a summer palace on the beach, called Klai Kangvol, "Far From Care" (ironically so, as the King was there in June of 1932 when word came that a revolution had ended the centuries-old absolute monarchy), and many members of the aristocracy built spacious holiday bungalows nearby. The less fortunate stayed at the Railway Hotel, where they enjoyed five-course Western meals, pony rides along the sand, and the use of a golf course advertised as "one of the finest east of Suez".

With the opening of roads to other, even closer resorts such as Pattaya on the other side of the gulf in the late 1950s, both Hua Hin and the Railway Hotel entered a period of gen-

teel decline. Even when this was reversed some 20 years later, the hotel seemed likely to be replaced by one of the more modern structures then being built. What saved it was "The Killing Fields", a film in which it was cast as Pnom Penh's Hotel Royale; the production company renovated the old teak structure with its airy verandahs and spacious rooms, to such effect that the new owners, the Central Hotel Group, was inspired to preserve it and put up a new building elsewhere in the compound.

Ever since it opened, one of the glories of the hotel was its garden, especially the huge topiary figures in the front area. Here generations of gardeners patiently clipped and shaped elephants, birds and assorted other figures, mostly using *Diospyros rhodocalyx* a tough native tree called *tako* in Thai and the Siamese Rough Bush in English. These were meticulously maintained in bad times as well as good and are still today one of Hua Hin's most popular attractions even among visitors who stay elsewhere.

The old-fashioned, formal arrangement of the front garden has also been restored, offering a rare glimpse of the sort of landscape favoured by grander Bangkok homes and palaces in the early 20th century, with clipped hedges of Bougainvillea and Ixora, beds of bright Cannas, neat pathways and fountains. A more contemporary tropical mixture has been planted on the beach side, but here, too, many of the original Rain trees, Plumerias and Flame trees still serve as reminders of the hotel's past.

Above: *The topiary garden of the old Railway Hotel, once a major resting place for travellers on the southern train line; Bougainvillea adds a touch of colour to the figure on the upper right.*

Right: *A formal pathway passing under a topiary elephant is lined with a hedge of Bougainvillea; the general layout is typical of many European-inspired gardens of the period. The pink flowering tree on the right is a Lagerstroemia. In the foreground are beds of Cannas which were popular in gardens of the period, and on either side, Norfolk Pines.*

Above: Bismarckia nobilis, *planted near an area devoted to exotic palms from all over the world.*

Left: *At the entrance to the Royal Garden Village, Coconut palms flourish in a lawn that leads down to one of the resort's several water features, planted with pink- and white-blooming Water Lilies.*

A LANDMARK SEASIDE GARDEN

Created by the noted Bensley Design Group, the landscape at the Royal Garden Village in the seaside resort of Hua Hin is seven years old, which in tropical terms means that it can now be enjoyed in its full, luxuriant maturity. The combination of sweeping vistas, secluded courtyards, imaginative water features and horticultural variety makes it a landmark achievement in garden design, one that offers useful lessons for both large-scale and more intimate arrangements.

Water plays a major role throughout the resort, most dramatically at the entrance where three large ponds are set in meticulously tended lawns. A wide range of aquatic plants grow in and around these, including pink- and white-blooming Nymphaea, *Thalia geniculata*, *Cyperus alternifolius*, *Typha angustifolia* and *Acrostichum aureum*, the Giant Mangrove fern, which has huge fronds that are brownish at the tips. This area also has a large number of

palms, ranging from the familiar Coconut to more exotic specimens like *Elaeis guineensis*, the African Oil palm, as well as the imposing *Ravenala madagascariensis*, popularly known as the Traveller's palm though in fact it belongs to the same family as the impressive Bird of Paradise (Strelitziaceae). Bougainvillea and flowering trees bring colour to the lawns; among the latter is *Crateva religiosa*, a native specimen, which produces a spectacular display of yellow and white blossoms during the hot season.

More useful, perhaps, to gardeners in search of ideas are the small courtyards, each of which offers a distinctive concept. One, for instance, is planted primarily with colourful Cordylines and Dracaenas, while another consists of Coconut palms rising from an area covered with riverbed pebbles and stones. There is a "White Garden" of shrubs and ground covers with white flowers or variegated leaves, as well as one centred on a small lily-studded pond.

More than 100 species are represented in the garden, constituting a virtual textbook of ornamental plants available in Thailand, and new ones are constantly being added. Among the palms, to mention a few, are the beautiful *Latania loddegesii* with silvery-blue leaves; *Prichardia pacifica*,

one of the handsomest of the fan palms; *Phoenix dactylifera*, the Date palm; and *Caryota mitis*, the graceful Fishtail palm. Flowering shrubs include the scented *Wrightia religiosa* and *Murraya paniculata*, Hibiscus in a wide range of colours, large and dwarf Ixora and *Eranthemum pulchellum* with sprays of mauve blossoms. Plants grown for their handsome foliage encompass numerous Dieffenbachia hybrids, Justicia, Codiaeum, Polyscias, Cordyline and Golden Crinum. *Artabotrys hexapetalus*, a creeper whose three-lobed flowers make up in fragrance what they lack in prominence, climbs over several of the upper terraces, and on others can be seen Allamanda, *Quisqualis indica* (Rangoon Creeper) and white *Beaumontia grandiflora*.

The collection of flowering trees is equally large — Plumeria in half a dozen hues, *Spathodea campanulata*, *Peltophorum pterocarpum* (the Yellow Flame tree), pink and yellow Tabebuia, Thevetia, *Brassaia actinophylla* (the Octopus tree) and *Callistemon lanceolatus* (the Bottlebrush), to make only a random selection.

Continually evolving, the Royal Garden Village succeeds both as a romantic tropical resort landscape and also as a major botanic collection.

Far left: *Water Poppy (Hydrocleys nymphoides) in a container with Chinese designs.*

Middle left: *Terracotta figure of a woman beside a Dieffenbachia.*

Left: *A Hindu god, adorned daily with Hibiscus flowers.*

Far left: *Water Lilies in a traditional jar with a lotus design.*

Middle left: *Figure of a Brahmin bull on a base of laterite.*

Left: *Glazed water jar, used to conceal a garden spotlight. On the left is Golden Duranta, on the right Justicia.*

Far left: *A small Thai-style pavilion sheltering traditional northern water jars.*

Middle left: *Hongsa, a mythological bird, in a bed of Justicia.*

Left: *Contemporary glazed water jar surrounded by Scindapsus, and behind, a Crinum Lily and broad-leafed Pandanus.*

Above: *A Thai pavilion in the garden outside the resort entrance, overlooking a Lily pond.*

Left: *Night-blooming pink Water Lilies, which remain open until the sun strikes them at mid-morning.*

Below: *European-style bridge over a waterway; on the left is a stand of Acrostichum aureum, the Giant Mangrove fern, and on the right Thalia geniculata. An old Thai ox cart serves as a garden ornament. The tree with the distinctive bark on the right is a Eucalyptus.*

Overleaf: *The Water Lily pond at the entrance to the resort. Floating on the surface is Pistia stratiotes, the Water Lettuce. The cream-coloured flowers in the background are those of Crateva adansonii, a tree native to the area which blooms spectacularly for a brief period in the hot season. On the left is Elaeis guineensis, the African Oil palm, the trunk of which provides a suitable place for orchids to grow.*

Below: *Coconut palms and a bed of dwarf Allamanda in the garden near the resort entrance; the yellow-flowering tree on the left,* Peltophorum pterocarpum, *popularly known as the Copperpod or the Yellow Flame tree, is planted in many Thai gardens.*

Opposite: *The Royal Garden Village swimming pool presents an inviting spectacle. Traveller's palms display their distinctive paddle-shaped leaves on the left, while a* Phoenix dactylifera *palm and Alocasias (Elephant's Ears) grow on an artificial island in the pool.*

GARDENING WITH NATURE

Above: The site of the Dusit Rayavadee Resort was originally a Coconut plantation, and most of the graceful palms have been incorporated into the garden design.

Opposite: Scaevola, a shrub with glossy-green leaves grows wild along the beaches of Southeast Asia and the Pacific; resistant to the most severe monsoon storms, it is a useful addition to seaside gardens of the region.

The concept for the 22-acre Dusit Rayavadee Resort in the southern province of Krabi came from M L Chainimit Navarat. An architect by profession, M L Chainimit owned a small bungalow on Phra Nang headland, a spectacular site bordered on two sides by towering limestone mountains and accessible only by sea. "I've travelled the world," he has been quoted as saying, "and seen a lot of places, but here is the most beautiful place I've been to."

The only accommodations on Phra Nang at the time were a few simple thatched huts. M L Chainimit's effort to upgrade standards by offering water and electricity drew criticism from some; nevertheless, he decided to create an up-market resort that would blend with the natural surroundings and meet the demands of most, if not all, environmentalists.

An investment partnership was formed with the Premier Group, a Bangkok-based conglomerate, additional land was acquired that included two more beaches and Four Aces Consultants Co Ltd was hired to do the planning and architectural design. Since the beaches

Above: *Two of the resort houses stand in a garden consisting almost entirely of graceful Coconut palms already growing on the site.*

and limestone cliffs are part of the Had Nopparat Thara National Park, sensitivity to the environment was a major consideration. Buildings were designed to blend into the landscape, a sophisticated water-treatment system was installed, allowing all waste water to be used for plants or for Lily ponds and fish pools and existing trees were retained whenever possible; aerial photographs taken before and after construction show that almost 100 per cent of the original trees still remain.

The success of these efforts was recognized by a Royal Gold Medal awarded by the Association of Siamese Architects, whose comment read in part, "Overall approach to design expressed sincerity and sympathy toward natural environment. Cultural sensitivity is also reflected in the adaptation of vernacular form. ...the engineering of the project also aims at minimizing the site contamination and energy consumption. A good model of conscientious development."

Simplicity is the keynote of the garden design. Coconut palms already growing in a plantation on the site still predominate, while other native seaside trees and shrubs include *Barringtonia asiatica*, *Hibiscus tiliaceus* (the Sea Hibiscus), *Calotropis gigantea* (the Crown Flower), Scaevola (Sea Lettuce), Pandanus (Screwpine) supported by aerial roots, and a local variety of Cycas (*prong* in Thai) which grows among the rocks along the coast. Well-adapted to conditions of drought and exposure to salty, monsoon winds, all these help avoid unnecessary fresh water consumption, as well as accentuating the garden's natural appearance. Introduced species like Heliconia, Hibiscus and Bougainvillea have become common in Southern Thailand and thus blend into the setting.

Left: The buildings of the Dusit Rayavadee are hexagonal structures that harmonize with the natural setting.

Below: Introduced ornamental plants, such as other palm trees and Heliconias, were carefully selected so that they complimented those already at the resort.

Below: *Imposing limestone cliffs provide a dramatic backdrop to the swimming pool.*

Opposite: *Phra Nang Bay offers some of Thailand's most spectacular marine scenery; the buildings of the resort have been designed to blend in as unobtrusively as possible and are scarcely visible from the air.*

Above: *A pathway leading to the main residence; the large clump on the left is a* Heliconia indica *cultivar with striped leaves, while the grey-leafed shrub below is* Justicia.

Opposite: *On a hillside adjacent to the garden,* Justicia fragilis *borders a path leading to a Buddhist shrine; the large-leafed climber is a* Philodendron, *while below are* Hymenocallis littoralis *and grey-leafed* Justicia.

Overleaf: *An old temple facade serves as a dramatic focal point. The steps on the right lead to a formal grassy entrance-way bordered by tall* Polyalthia longifolia pendula. *The slope in the foreground is planted with a mixture of palms, native trees,* Philodendrons, *ferns and variegated* Acorus gramineus.

A GARDEN ON THE ANDAMAN SEA

The Phuket estate of M L Tri Devakul, a prominent architect, began with a single thatched-roof house on a rocky hillside with a spectacular view of the Andaman Sea. Over the years since it has expanded into a diverse collection of buildings, linked by now-mature gardens of tropical plants and trees that have steadily changed in design and atmosphere along with the man-made features.

As the gardens grew in size and variety, two problems common to most seaside properties had to be confronted. One was a lack of water in sufficient quantities to support introduced ornamentals during the dry season; another was the strong, salty winds that sweep in during the moonsoon months between July and October with disastrous effect on more tender specimens. The water shortage was alleviated by incorporating a reservoir into the landscape design and by drip-system watering of some areas. The monsoon challenge was met by installing canvas blinds along a loggia to protect an inner garden during storms and

by careful selection of trees and shrubs for more exposed places. Bougainvillea, for example, thrives in such locations, and so do such trees as *Terminalia catappa* (the Sea Almond), *Casuarina equisetifolia* (the Sea Oak), *Barringtonia asiatica* (a native tree with large, handsome, glossy leaves), and *Hibiscus tiliaceus* (the Sea Hibiscus), as well as shrubs like Scaevola, or Sea Lettuce, *Crinum asiaticum*, and a tough variety of Pandanus popularly called the Screwpine. Some of these already growing on the site were incorporated into the garden design, while others were brought in to create more effective wind screens.

Like the various buildings, each of the garden areas has a distinctive atmosphere. There is a formal aspect to a grassy entrance walkway from the parking area, provided by flanking rows of tall *Polyalthia longifolia pendula*, an evergreen tree with long narrow leaves that assumes a stately, cypress-like shape. A central garden also has a formal series of pools extending down the hillside but is more jungly in general appearance, with dense plantings of Aglaonema, Dieffenbachia, Asplenium (Bird's Nest ferns), *Alpinia purpurata* (Red Ginger), *Costus speciosus* (Crepe Ginger), Alocasia (Elephant's Ear), Codiaeum, huge

Above: An over-sized chair from northern Thailand sits on this terrace overlooking a garden with a jungle-like atmosphere. Stag's Horn ferns (Platycerium coronarium) and Bird's Nest ferns (Asplenium nidus) grow on some of the trees, while a Philodendron climbs up one of the pillars.

Opposite: Simple furniture and terracotta tiles accentuate the atmosphere of this serene upper terrace. Philodendrons clamber up one of the trees overlooking the fishpond in the centre. The flame-like wooden pieces, called chofah, are styalized carvings of birds used on the roofs of Thai temples and palaces; the old cannon was found in Phuket, and now guards the corner of the terrace.

Below: *Roots of a wild Ficus wrap around a huge boulder along a pathway leading to the owner's gallery of sculptures, one of which can be seen on the lower terrace. Through the trees behind can be glimpsed the salt-water swimming pool and the ever-present vista of the sea.*

Left: The sculpture gallery affords panoramic views of the Andaman Sea; on the left is a stand of wild Pandanus.

Below: Along a gallery connecting various houses, canvas blinds can be lowered during strong monsoon winds to protect garden areas behind.

Bottom: Existing trees and boulders have been incorporated into the design of several parts of the garden.

tands of *Heliconia indica* with striped leaves nd assorted Philodendrons clambering up ative trees.

On a sunnier adjacent slope where a Buddhist shrine stands, colourful ground overs and such flowering trees and shrubs s Plumeria, *Delonix regia* (Flame tree), *Bixa orellana* (Lipstick tree), Hibiscus, *Tecoma stans* (Yellow Bells) and Mussaenda have been added to the Cashew Nut trees nd Coconut palms already growing there, vhile yet another area is largely devoted to

assorted Heliconias. Wild Ficus trees wrap their roots picturesquely around a huge boulder along a flight of steps near a gallery displaying some of the owner's sculptures, and Pandanus with aerial roots shelter a terrace near the salt-water swimming pool built amid the rocks at the lower level.

The sea is visible from almost every point in this garden of changing vistas, first glimpsed as a flash of blue through trees from the entrance, finally as a panorama from any of the terraces below the loggia.

Below: *A terrace beside the swimming pool; the tree on the right is* Terminalia catappa, *the Sea Almond, which can withstand even the strongest monsoon winds.*

Right: *Views of both sea and pool are provided by this terrace, shaded by a Sea Almond tree; all the stonework here and elsewhere was done by a skilled mason on the owner's staff.*

Below: *A massed planting of Hymenocallis littoralis, the Spider Lily, lines a stairway leading down to the swimming pool; the tree is Barringtonia asiatica, native to the region, while Bougainvillea is planted below the verandah of the house. All three are particularly resistant to strong winds from the sea.*

Above: *A traditional northern Thai woodcarving adorns the gable of this structure, used for entertaining. Bougainvillea and* Hymenocallis littoralis *are planted below.*

Left: *Pandanus, commonly called the Seashore Screwpine, displays its impressive aerial roots on one side of the pool; resistant to salty sea winds, it is ideally suited for such exposed locations.*

Below: *Masses of Bougainvillea frame the salt-water pool, which incorporates existing boulders in its design; also incorporated was the hardy* Terminalia catappa, *which was already growing on the site.*

NORTHERN THAILAND

Rolling hills, mountains that rise to heights of more than 2,000 metres, lush valleys watered by rivers and streams—these are the physical characteristics of northern Thailand. Bordered by Burma and Laos, the area is geographically and culturally distinct from the rest of Thailand. The lower mountains were once covered by extensive forests of Teak, and when the earliest Thai groups migrated south from China, they established principalities in the fertile valleys. Eventually, the Lanna kingdom centred around Chiang Mai was founded in the mid-13th century. Until the railway line reached Chiang Mai in the early 1920s, the region was isolated from the rest of the country, and only in recent years has it become a major tourist destination as well as a popular place among Thais to build holiday homes.

Gardeners in the north, especially those accustomed to the monotonously flat terrain of the Central Plains, enjoy a number of advantages. The varied topography encourages the creation of more interesting landscapes, while the cool winter weather allows the cultivation of many ornamentals that can be grown only with effort, if at all, at lower altitudes.

Opposite: *A thatched-roof house provides a rustic touch to the Pong Yang Garden Village, one of several resorts that have been established in the hills above Chiang Mai. Among the native trees incorporated into the garden design is the Teak (Tectona grandis) growing in the foreground; wild northern Orchids grow on its trunk.*

Overleaf: *Tall cypress-like Cupressus (right), beds and borders of Roses and a mountainous backdrop give the Napa Doi estate in the north an exotic appeal to visitors from sea-level Bangkok, while local colour is provided by a Thai-style pavilion and buildings with distinctive northern Thai roofs. A mass of Bougainvillea blooms on the left while on the right can be seen the spiky white leaves of a large Agave.*

However, there are certain horticultural drawbacks. During the summer between March and June, valley temperatures can be intense—even hotter than in Bangkok—and adequate water can be a problem. Moreover the soil on many slopes is thin, making it necessary to bring in large amounts of topsoil and manure before a really luxuriant garden can be established. During the rainy season from July to October, some riverside sites are prone to flooding. Gardening for a substantial part of the year thus requires intensive effort, more perhaps than can be expended on a home occupied by its owners for only occasional visits, unless they have reliable help.

Despite these problems, there has been a remarkable increase of notable northern gardens. Some of the earliest were established along the banks of the Ping River, where there is both a water supply and rich soil as well as scenic views of mountains. Even more enticing opportunities came a decade or so ago when a road was built through the Mae Sa Valley, 30 kilometres outside Chiang Mai, opening for development one of the most beautiful areas in the region. Orchid nurseries and resorts were opened along the road, soon followed by housing estates and private homes.

Many of the Mae Sa projects resemble those found in the hill stations established by homesick colonials in Malaysia and Indonesia: They feature Western-style bungalows and the gardens are planted primarily with temperate-zone specimens like Salvia, Dahlias, Chrysanthemums and, above all, Roses.

As more imaginative gardeners moved into the valley, however, other types of landscapes began to appear, composed of plants that definitely qualified as tropical but that grew with remarkable vigour in the cool fresh air—Heliconias, for example, as well as Impatiens, Coleus, Euphorbia and such exotics as the Jade Vine and the New Guinea Creeper.

Out of this combination of countryside, weather and creativity, together with the constant introduction of new plant materials, have emerged some of Thailand's best contemporary gardens.

Left: A modernistic chalet with northern Thai decorations stands near towering stands of native bamboo in a northern estate near Chiang Rai.

Above right: The estate planting includes red Ixora, golden Duranta repens, Cycads and Impatiens.

Right: Early morning mist shrouds this garden arrangement along a pebble path; among the flowering plants are Bougainvillea and Ixora. Rhapis palms grow close to the house.

Right: *Both native and hybrid Orchids have become almost synonymous with Thailand. Here is a selection photographed in northern gardens, including on right* Dendrobium fredrichsiana.

Far right: Dendrobium lindleyi.

Right: *Ascocentrum hybrid.*

Far right: Vanda coerulea.

Right: *Vanda hybrid.*

Far right: *Ascocentrum hybrid.*

Far Left: Dendrobium 'Mme Pompadour'.

Left: Dendrobium hybrid.

Far left: Brassiolaeliocattleya 'Lucky Strike'.

Left: Brassiolaeliocattleya 'Alma Kee'.

Far left: Catteleya 'Queen Sirikit'.

Left: Rhyncostylus hybrid.

Overleaf: Bold spiky Agave americana stand out against the carefully tended lawn of the Napa Doi housing estate near Chiang Mai, which also includes a stream that provides water year round for the garden.

Above: *A bed of annual Cleomes add a mass of colour to the gardens at the Lanna resort. In the background a row of tall* Cupressus sempervirens *reach up into the sky.*

Opposite: *A mass planting of Cycas lends a dramatic note to the Lanna garden; in the background are Phoenix palms and* Beaucarnea recurvata, *popularly called the "Pony-tail Palm".*

GARDENS FOR ESCAPE

Until a decade or so ago, when Bangkok residents sought relief from the city's heat and pollution, they headed for such established seaside retreats as Pattaya and Hua Hin or, in the case of the more affluent, for cooler climates in distant Europe and North America. Increasingly, however, more and more have been going to northern Thailand, where a number of unusual resort landscapes have been created in the hills just outside Chiang Mai.

Some of the most beautiful of these are located on a road that was opened in the 1980s, first to the Mae Sa Valley and then continuing on through several other similarly scenic areas. The facilities include bungalows, often of rustic appearance but offering modern comforts, restaurants and extensive gardens that, during winter months, are ablaze with colourful temperate annuals seldom seen at lower elevations. Formal landscape designs are favoured by some, while others make imaginative use of the natural topography and native trees and plants.

Below: *On the right of this small water feature at Pong Yang Garden Village is a mass* Cuphea miniata, *while on the left are* Impatiens. *The lacy plant growing out of the rock below is* Phyllanthus myrtifolius.

Opposite: *The Pong Yang Garden Village utilises vernacular items in its tropical setting. Here, ferns provide a bower for a traditional water jar; the low plant with green and white leaves on the left is* Pilea cardieri.

At Pong Yang Garden Village, for example, a huge stand of indigenous Bamboo grows at the entrance to a pathway leading to the main building, artfully planted with both local and introduced species. The same atmosphere prevails over the resort's several levels, from most of which there is a view of a spectacular waterfall that cascades even in the driest months. Neatly clipped hedges of a variety of *Duranta repens* that has bright golden leaves in full sunlight contrast with colour-ful Bougainvillea, flowering shrubs, more of the Bamboo that grows in the region and some wild trees such as a Bauhinia species that produces masses of small, white flowers during the hot season. Various artifacts like old northern ox carts and large water jars are strategically placed here and there in the garden.

The Lanna Resort is more formal, with sweeping lawns and numerous clipped specimens, among them Bougainvillea, *Acalypha wilkesiana*, Golden Duranta and

Above: A stand of native Bamboo rises near a pavilion at Pong Yang; the hedge is Duranta repens.

Right: The yellow-leaf variety of Duranta repens, called Golden Tea by Thais, can be clipped into tight hedges or massed beds. The tall plants are Dracaena loureiri, a native plant, and the ox cart is decorated with pots of red Euphorbia pulcherrima. In the background can be seen a forest of wild Bamboos.

Left: Euphorbia pulcherrima *with white bracts flowers on the left, while the spiky plant nearby is* Agave angustifolia, *popularly known as the Century Plant.*

Right: *At Pong Yang Garden Village, an old ox cart is displayed against a background of Bougainvillea and the surrounding forest.*

Below: *A thatched-roof house lends a rustic touch to the natural-looking garden that has been created at Pong Yang.*

Ficus. Members of the Coniferae family such as tall, slender *Cupressus sempervirens* and bushy, cedar-like *Thuja orientalis*, which grow well in the hills, provide an exotic, European touch for Thai visitors, as do seasonal beds of annuals like Salvia, Cleome and Marigolds. Yellow-flowering *Cassia siamea* bloom for most of the year along a stream that runs behind the restaurant, while a mass planting of Cycas lends a dramatic note against the thickly forested hills that rise around the resort's valley setting.

The most popular season for visiting these northern resorts is between November and the end of February, when temperatures are lowest and the gardens are ablaze with temperate-zone flowers only seen elsewhere in the country as cut specimens. Even familiar trees and shrubs seem to grow larger and bloom more profusely in the cool mountain air. Summers in the valleys can be hot, but with relatively low humidity it is still comfortable for strolls along the pathways past the streams that run year round through most of the landscapes. These resort gardens are also constantly introducing new plants and discovering ways to enhance the horticultural beauty of these holiday destinations.

Right: Cassia siamea offer frequent displays of bright yellow flowers at the Lanna resort.

Below: Also at the Lanna resort, Bougainvilleas are trained and clipped into standards; tall, slender Cupressus sempervirens add a European touch to the garden.

Below: Cassia siamea *(left), Bougainvillea and clipped hedges of golden* Duranta repens *bring almost continual colour to the Lanna Resort.*

Above: *Beds of such temperate-zone annuals as Salvia and Marigolds are popular with Thai visitors from lower elevations.*

Left: *A formal arrangement of clipped Ficus trees, golden Duranta repens and Cupressus sempervirens lines one of the resort's pathways.*

Overleaf: *The main lawn of the resort; the bright leaves on the right are Acalypha wilkesiana, while the yellow is golden Duranta repens. From any angle guests have a view of jungled hills that surround the resort.*

A NORTHERN RESORT

Left: *A large bed is planted with a cultivar of* Heliconia indica, *grown for foliage rather than flowers. Behind it,* Spathodea campanulata, *the African Tulip tree, blooms near one of the resort structures.*

Opposite: *Colour and leaf variety are achieved in a grassy area below the main building through beds of low-growing* Rhoeo discolor, *variegated* Dianella ensifolia *and spiky green and yellow Sansivieria. The tree in the centre is* Millingtonia hortensis, *popularly called the Indian Cork Tree.*

The Regent, a collection of structures that spills down the slopes of a picturesque valley in the Mae Rim District, about 30 kilometres from Chiang Mai, is a relatively new resort. Already, however, the resort's extensive gardens designed by the Bangkok-based Bensley Design Group have attracted widespread interest and admiration.

The Bensley Design Group has created landscapes for other properties in Thailand as well as a number in Bali. It was perhaps their experience in the latter that led to the incorporation of terraced rice fields into the Regent concept. These working fields occupy most of the lower valley and extend right up to the resort's guest pavilions. Kept supplied with water from a nearby local reservoir during the long dry season, they produce crops several times a year.

Elsewhere, the pavilions and other hotel facilities are linked by luxuriant tropical gardens. Certain specimens are repeated throughout the resort in effective massed plantings, among them *Alocasia macrorrhizos*, the so-called Elephant's Ear with huge heart-shaped leaves; two

varieties of Crinum, one the native *C. Asiaticum* with long, broad leaves and stalks of fragrant flowers and another, smaller type of more recent introduction with bright gold leaves; a Heliconia cultivar grown for its dark red foliage; Acalyphas in bright colours and leaf forms; *Hymenocallis littoralis*, popularly known as the Spider Lily; Spathiphyllums with white spathes; and Sansevierias with both variegated and pure silver leaves. Stands of Golden Bamboo, a variety of *Dracaena fragrans* with green and gold striped leaves, and assorted flowering Bananas provide further colour accents, while Torch Gingers (*Etlingera elatoir*), Bird's Nest ferns (*Asplenium nidus*) and Stag's Horn ferns (*Platycerium coronarium*) contribute to the jungle-like effect. In the cooler, winter months, some beds are planted with such temperate annuals as Zinnia, Celosia and Salvia.

A more formal water garden provides a contrast along one side of the open lobby pavilion, with day- and night-blooming Nymphaea and mauve-flowering *Thalia geniculata*, sometimes called the Water Canna; another, is planted solely with *Typha angustifolia* that rise more than a metre above the water level.

Because many of the original forest trees were retained on the site, these help to give the gardens a mature appearance. To these have been added such flowering species as *Spathodea campanulata*, *Delonix regia*, Millingtonia and Plumeria in a number of different colours.

Above: Contrasting colours and leaf textures are created through massed plantings of ground covers and both foliage and flowering shrubs. Young flowering trees which will eventually become much larger have been planted throughout the resort.

Below: In the foreground is a stand of Golden Bamboo, while the beds behind are planted with a variety of Crinum on which the leaves are gold in full or partial sunlight. The wooden lantern in the foreground was made by a Chiang Mai craftsman.

A GARDEN OF HELICONIAS

Heliconias, natives of the American tropics, were only one of many components in the original design for this garden on the bank of the Ping River just outside Chiang Mai. Of equal importance were a large number of mature Plumerias acquired from a local nursery, as well as a wide variety of flowering shrubs and trees densely planted to provide maximum privacy for each of the three Thai-style residences on the property as well as to create constantly changing vistas along the winding pathways.

During installation of the garden, however, the residents became increasingly interested in the huge Heliconia family, which numbers approximately 250 species and almost as many forms or cultivars. Contact was made with Mark Collins, owner of the famous Eden Farms in Hilo, Hawaii, and one of the acknowledged experts in the field, and this led not only to the introduction of many varieties that had never before been tried in Thai gardens but also eventually to the formation of a company, Siam Mariposa, for the purpose of growing

Opposite: A cultivar of Heliconia caribaea Lamarck, *which can grow up to heights of six metres.*

Below: A view of the swimming pool and one of the houses: In addition to the Heliconia collection, the garden contains many other exotic tropical plants. Here, the planting in the foreground includes bright-red Ixora javanica, Alpinia purpurata (Red Ginger), variegated Duranta repens and Crinum amabile; a mass of Ficus trees softens the waterfall on the opposite side of the pool.

Below: Heliconia stricta cv. 'Firebird', *one of the most popular Heliconias grown for the cut-flower market.*

Above left: Heliconia psittacorum cv. 'St. Vincent Red'.

Above centre: Heliconia x nickeriensis Maas & deRooij (H. psittacorum x H. marginata).

Above right: Heliconia orthotricha cv. 'Total Eclipse'. *This heliconia was introduced to Thailand in this garden.*

Below: *Golden Bamboo grows on the right of the entrance stairs, while on the left is* Congea tomentosa, *a creeper native to northern Thailand; the white flowers below are* Gardenia jasminoides.

Opposite: *The breezy verandah of this house has a panoramic view of the Ping River; over the railing grow* Congea tomentosa *and* Mucuna bennetti, *while potted Bougainvillea provide colour.*

Top: Mucuna bennetti, *the striking New Guinea Creeper. It grows along a trellis in the front of the main house and blooms most spectacularly in October.*

Above: *A stand of Golden Bamboo outside one of the houses.*

Heliconias commercially for export as cut flowers. Shortly after the garden's completion, a serious flood resulted in the loss of many of the Plumerias; by this time, though, the Heliconia collection had grown to the point where the plants already predominated in most areas and give the landscape its highly distinctive character.

A rectangular plot lying between the river and a road, the site was originally a Longan plantation. Highly prized in the north for their lychee-like fruit, these low-growing trees (known botanically as *Dimocarpus longan*, in Thai *lamyai*) are not very suitable for ornamental gardens due to the dense shade they cast; most were therefore removed, though a few were retained for screening purposes until newer, more decorative specimens like *Delonix regia* (Flame tree), *Samanea saman* (Rain tree), Erythrina (Tiger's Claw), *Tabebuia rosea* (Pink Trumpet tree) *Spathodea Campanulata* (African Tulip tree) and several varieties of Ficus reached maturity.

Various levels are achieved through a series of massed plantings on mounded areas, the components selected on the basis of colour; a green and gold arrangement, for example, includes an *Erythrina variegata* with brightly patterned leaves, yellow Allamanda, variegated Alpinia and assorted Codiaeum, while on another the predominant colours are pink and white. Huge stones from the Mekong River bed are also incorporated into the garden design and used to create a natural-looking waterfall beside the swimming pool.

The growing Heliconia collection now includes specimens of all the major varieties, from the huge *caribaea* to the "Dwarf Jamaica" of the *striata* group. Since new ones are constantly being added, any listing is certain to be incomplete, but of particular interest to local collectors are some handsome *orthotrichas* (one, popularly called "Total Eclipse" has very dark purple inforescences), *strictas*, and *acuminatas*, all as yet unfamiliar to Thai landscapes.

Left: *View of the swimming pool from the verandah; the smaller Heliconias below are* H. psittacorum *cultivars, while the taller ones are* H. caribaea. *The tree with the green and gold leaves in the background is* Erythrina variegata, *while the feathery wild Bamboo on the left was planted to screen the property from a road.*

Above left: *A form of* Musa coccinea, *the Red-flowering Banana.*

Above centre: *A pink-flowering cultivar of* Alpinia purpurata.

Above right: Alpinia purpurata, *popularly called Red Ginger.*

Below: *On the right is* Strongylodon macrobotrys, *the spectacular Jade Vine, a native of the Philippines and one of the most extraordinary vines in the world. On the left in a planting devoted to pink and white shrubs is* Pithecellobium dulce, *on which the new leaves are pink or snow-white when grown in full sun.*

A RUSTIC RETREAT

Above: *A breezy verandah on one of the houses offers protection for a variety of potted plants; the low table, known as a kantoke, is traditional to northern Thailand.*

Opposite: *Tall stands of native bamboo frame the entrance steps to the main house; in pots below are Asplenium nidus (Bird's Nest ferns), while a species of wild northern Orchid grows on the right. The narrow trunks on the left are Betel Nut palms.*

Patrapara Charusorn's house and garden, about an hour's drive from Chiang Mai, first reveals itself as a mass of greenery set like an island in a sea of rice fields reached by an unpaved country lane. This same rural atmosphere is also prevalent within the compound, where the rustic, though comfortable, wooden houses afford glimpses through the trees of fields that merge with the boundary lines to suggest a unity of garden and countryside.

The owner comes from a family of plant lovers—her brother is one of Thailand's best-known landscape designers—and what began as a Chiang Mai retreat has become a place where she now spends much of her time. The three houses on the property are called Fish, Rabbit and Bird, and each is decorated with carved figures and other pieces of folk art appropriate to the particular name; all are airy structures with spacious verandahs overlooking the garden. "I like to look at the plants," Khun Patrapara says. "I always feel happy when I do and never lonely, even when I'm here all alone."

The most prominent garden features are several stands of huge native Bamboo, which were already growing on the site and provide shade as well as dramatic focal points. Alpinias and Heliconias are planted along one side of the main house; among the latter is a remarkably healthy stand of *H. chartacea*, a variety popularly known as "Sexy Pink" that has spectacular pendulous pink and red bracts. Wild Orchids of the region grow on many of the trees, bursting into sprays of blossoms during the hot season between March and May, while over a pond that serves as a reservoir an enormous white Calliandra spreads its branches, usually covered with snowball-like flowers.

Also planted around the pond is *Elaeocarpus hygrophilus Kurtz*, a small native tree known in Thai as *ma-kok nam*, which produces both plum-like fruit and fragrant flowers. (Bangkok, "village of the *kok* trees", acquired its name from the fact that large numbers once grew there along the banks of the Chao Phraya River.) Among the vines that clamber up a support in the garden is a *Mucuna bennetti*, the New Guinea Creeper, which once a year (usually in October) puts forth dazzling clusters of red-orange flowers, as well as *Jasminium rex*, a slender creeper with large white star-shaped flowers.

A bridge across a year-round stream leads to an area which serves as a nursery, where pots of shade-loving plants grow under the trees and Bamboo clumps. In atmosphere, this seems a part of the main garden, as it has sitting areas where one can relax.

Below: *A pond serves as a reservoir for the garden; on the right is some of the wild Bamboo that once filled the site, while in the background are rice fields that still surround it.*

Opposite: *A sitting area in the garden, shaded by native trees and wild Bamboo. Wild ferns grow at the base of the bamboos.*

A COLLECTOR'S GARDEN

Above: Cut sprays of orchids are placed in tall northern drums to add a festive touch for a party.

Opposite: A Balinese statue with a carefully-nurtured patina of moss and decorated with pink Hibiscus blossoms from the garden, stands sentinel at the entrance of the Von Boehm's traditional Thai home; on the right you can see a mass planting of Cordyline varieties, with Pilea as a ground cover.

Dieter and Susie Von Boehm originally built their house overlooking Chiang Mai's Ping River as a holiday retreat, going there only when they had free time from a busy life in Bangkok and business postings abroad. "It was impossible to really do much in the way of serious gardening," Mr Von Boehm says. "We'd bring plants back from places where we lived or travelled, put them in, and pray they'd make it through the next dry season or the next flood. Quite often they didn't." With retirement a few years ago, however, the Von Boehms moved full-time to the property, and now what might be called a true collector's garden shows the effect of what love and care may bring.

A large park-like area contains those specimens that managed to survive the early days of benign neglect—actually a surprising number considering the prolonged dry months that Chiang Mai gardens are subjected to from November through April—as well as others that have been installed more recently. While some were acquired in local nurseries, many came

Right: Mucuna bennetti, *popularly known as the New Guinea Creeper, blooms in October and November in the north.*

Middle right: Gustavia superba, *known in Thailand as the "Lotus Flower", is a slow-growing shrub that can become a small tree.*

Far right: Persea americana, *the Avocado Pear, is still relatively uncommon in Thailand, particularly in gardens.*

Right: Clusia, *a native of Central and South America with glossy green leaves, occasionally produces this large flower.*

Middle right: Thunbergia erecta *is a dependable shrub which usually has deep-purple flowers; there is also a white variety.*

Far right: Solanum wrightii, *commonly called the Potato tree, is seldom seen in Thai gardens.*

Right: *This citrus tree (*Citrus medica*), brought as a seedling from Java, produces large, lemon-like fruit that are unfortunately inedible.*

Middle right: *Fragrant* Gardenia jasminoides *is planted near the entrance of both houses on the Von Boehm property.*

Left: *This variety of Coral Tree,* Erythrina fusca, *produces ruby-red flowers and leaves at the same time.*

from other countries like Indonesia and Australia in the form of seeds or cuttings and are thus of particular interest to any plant lover who delights in horticultural variety and oddity.

Towering over a mixed bed of unusual Codiaeums, red and white Poinsettias, scarlet Mussaenda and other shrubs with colourful flowers or foliage is a huge *Solanum wrightii*: Commonly called the Potato tree, (although it is a member of the Tomato family from Brazil), it has large rich purple-blue flowers and is seldom seen in Thai gardens. Other specimens include *Amherstia nobilis*, called by some "the world's most beautiful flowering tree", a native of neighbouring Burma but as yet too young to bring forth its first spectacular display of coral-pink flower clusters; *Kigelia pinnata*, commonly called the Sausage tree, also still immature but one day expected to produce the long strange-looking hanging fruits responsible for its popular name;

several already productive avocado trees; and a stand of special Bananas from Israel. *Congea tomentosa*, a climber native to the region, offers a regular winter display of velvety pink and white bracts, while assorted Bougainvilleas provide splashes of vivid colour along the river bank.

Areas around two northern-style houses are planted more intimately with assorted Hibiscus, Gardenias and other flowering shrubs and, in shadier areas, ornamentals with strikingly-patterned leaves such as Calatheas, Marantas and Aglaonemas.

Above: *Specimens in the main gardens include* Bambusa ventricosa, *popularly called the Buddha's Belly Bamboo (foreground), white and red* Euphorbia pulcherrima (Poinsettia) *and* Bougainvillea.

Left: *Shrubs in this bed include, from left to right,* Euphorbia pulcherrima, Codiaeum *in a variety of colours and* Justicia fragilis, *while among the trees in the background are* Plumeria *and* Solanum wrightii.

Opposite: *An old rice granary converted into a guest house in the Von Boehm garden has a carved gable and a rooftop decoration known as a galae, characteristic of houses in the Chiang Mai area. The planting in front includes fragrant White Ginger* (Hedychium coronarium), Coleus, Roses *and* Ophiopogon.

Above: *A Burmese-style image of a goddess who according to legend wrung water from her hair stands in front of the yellow-flowered* Tecoma stans, *popularly called Golden Bells.*

Left: *Along the entrance stairs is a modern adaptation of a traditional serpent balustrade; an old boat hewn from a single teak log (foreground) is planted with temperate annuals such as Petunias and Carnations. The trees on either side of the stairs are Millingtonia, an old Thai favourite with fragrant white flowers, while the plant with gold and green leaves at the foot of the stairs is the Song of India (Draecena reflexa).*

TWO NORTHERN HOLIDAY GARDENS

Few of the holiday homes near Chiang Mai match the beauty of the one built by Suchin and Rujiraporn Wanglee and Nitthi Sthapitanond, partners in a prominent firm that offers architectural, interior design and landscaping services. Thanks to their comprehensive skills, it was only to be expected that the neighbouring houses and gardens they created in an estate called Baan Rim Thai Sai Thorn would be highly distinctive.

Confirmation of this comes along the entrance drive shared by the houses, where *Cymbopogon citratus* has been planted in large beds. Popularly known as Lemon Grass, this is a staple in Thai cooking but proves equally effective as an ornamental plant with its slender, grass-like foliage that rises several feet high and merges to form an almost solid cover. Another practical touch in the Wanglee garden is a bed in the centre of the main lawn devoted to decorative cabbage plants, ranging in colour from pale green to deep purple.

Above and left: *Decorative cabbages and other vegetables are given a place of honour in the back lawn, changed periodically as they mature. Planted near the house is a bed of Lemon Grass (Cymbopogon citratus) which also serves an ornamental as well as a practical purpose.*

Above: On a wooden deck overlooking a pond, an old teak boat is planted with multi-coloured creeping Lantana and water jars with Lotus. In and around the pond are tall Typha angustifolia, Crinum Lilies and Papyrus.

In front of the Wanglee house, an old boat hewn from a hollowed-out tree trunk is planted with a seasonal display of temperate annuals, while the entrance steps are flanked with a luxuriant arrangement that includes Heliconia, *Dracaena reflexa* (the green and gold Song of India), *Murraya paniculata* (Mock Orange) and Phoenix palms. Among the flowering trees are *Millingtonia hortensis* (the Cork tree), *Spathodea campanulata* (African Tulip tree), *Gliricidia sepium* (the pale pink flowers of which are used in Thai cuisine), *Erythrina variegata* (the Coral tree), *Melia azedarach* (Persian Lilac) and *Tecoma stans* (Golden Bells). A wooden deck on one side of the house overlooks a water garden that contains *Typha angustifolia*, Egyptian Papyrus, *Thalia geniculata* (sometimes called the Water Canna, with tall clusters of purple flowers), and the culinary herb *Pandanus amaryllifolius*.

The house built by Professor Nitthi is a multi-roofed structure in a walled com-

Below: *The multi-roofed house of Khun Nitthi Sthapitanond is reminiscent of Burmese architecture; in the foreground, Lemon Grass has been used as a decorative bedding plant.*

pound reminiscent of those seen in Bali. A mass of yellow-blooming *Galphimia glauca* is planted just outside a pair of carved wooden doors, which lead to a small courtyard surrounded by beds of *Gardenia jasminoides* and *Brunfelsia pauciflora 'floribunda compacta'* (formerly called *Brunfelsia eximia*). The latter is whimsically known as the "Yesterday-Today-and-Tomorrow Plant" since its flowers change from mauve to white over the course of several days.

Another courtyard behind is centred on a formal pool with such aquatic specimens as Water Lilies, *Hydrocleys nymphoides* (Water Poppy) and *Thalia geniculata*. A pavilion with rustic, hand-carved pillars stands at one end of the pool and, at the other, a northern-style *singha*, or mythical lion, against a backdrop of tall *Etlingera elatior*.

Final evidence of the originality of these two gardens can be found outside the walls of Professor Nitthi's house, where two rice barns stand atop high posts, minus the tiles that once covered their roofs. Instead of being restored these will eventually serve as unusual supports for *Congea tomentosa*, a creeper with dusty-pink flowers that has already reached the top in several places.

Above: The interior courtyard of Khun Nitthi's house includes a formal pool with assorted water plants, overlooked by a contemporary singha, or sacred guardian lion. Against the house is a tall stand of Torch Ginger (Etlingera elatior), while the feathery water cover in the foreground is Myriophyllum aquaticum.

Right: An old rice granary and a spirit house stand outside the house compound; the flowering tree is a Cassia bakeriana, the Pink Shower tree.

Far right: An old northern house with a decorative gable.

A VALLEY GARDEN

When Chare Chutharatkul first acquired his property in the picturesque Samuang District of Chiang Mai, it consisted largely of rice fields, well watered by three year-round streams, and was surrounded by thickly-forested hills. Over the years since, he and Kanisorn Wuthinon, a Chiang Mai-based designer, have transformed the site into a remarkable garden with lakes and pools and a wide choice of landscape moods.

The front terrace of the house looks out over a series of pools on different levels, green lawns, and what appears from a distance to be sculpted masses of colour. The latter effect has been achieved through the use of meticulously clipped shrubs and trees with varied foliage, some standing alone and others blending into one another to create intriguing combinations. Among the plants used here are *Carissa macrocarpa 'Humphreyi Variegata'*, a green and white shrub with small leaves; bright red and bronze *Acalypha wilkesiana*; dwarf Ixora; *Hamelia patens*, the "Fire Bush", with pale green leaves and small, red-orange flowers;

Left: *A Lily pond with a simple bridge, one of several that provide water for the garden as well as visual appeal.*

Below: *Set in a valley, the garden offers a wide range of colour, partly through foliage shrubs like Golden Duranta and red Acalypha and partly through flowering varieties like the pink Calliandra on the right. The cedar-like trees are Thuja orientalis.*

Overleaf: *The spectacular view from the terrace of the house reveals a soothing landscape composed of water, stones, and contrasting colours; growing over the pebbled areas in the foreground is Juniperus.*

variegated Hibiscus with pink and white leaves; golden *Duranta repens*; purple-flowering *Thunbergia erecta*; *Barlaria cristata*; *Sanchezia nobilis*, with dark green leaves that are boldly striped with yellow; and assorted Ficus of the smaller types with thick rounded leaves. *Phyllanthus myrtifolius*, a low-growing plant with feathery leaves, droops over rocks and softens the edges of the assorted pools.

Also incorporated into this area are such Coniferae as *Thuja orientalis*, several species of Juniperus and *Cupressus sempervirens*. Near the pathway leading up to the house are beds of Cleome, Phlox, Salvia, Carnations and other annuals that will grow at this elevation for a substantial part of the year.

A large assortment of flowering trees and shrubs can be seen in less formal parts of the garden, among them *Calliandra surinamensis*, which regularly produces masses of pink and white powder-puff blooms; *Solanum wrightii*, the Potato tree, with mauve-coloured flowers; *Tecoma stans*, popularly known as Golden Bells; *Lagerstroemia speciosa*, the Pride of India; fragrant *Wrightia religiosa*; and *Clerodendrum quadriloculare*, a sizeable shrub with dark green and purple leaves and periodic

Above: *Beds of annuals and such trees as Juniperus and Thuja orientalis lend a European atmosphere to some parts of the spacious garden.*

Left: *A pathway of irregular stones leads through a cover of Ophiopogon japonicus to the front terrace.*

Left: *The house, carefully planned by the owner to offer views of the garden from all sides.*

Below: *A large Agave americana rises from a mixed bed of temperate annuals that includes Daisies, Carnations, Salvia and Cleome.*

Above: *An artful waterfall created with local stones. The tall clipped shrubs in the background are mauve and white flowering Barleria, while the one on the right is a native specimen already growing along the bed of the stream that flows through the garden.*

Left: *A marshy area behind the house is planted with assorted water-loving plants such as* Papyrus, Cyperus alternifolius *and low-growing* Pandanus amaryllifolius.

Below: *A venerable wild* Ficus, *one of the many native specimens already growing on the site that Khun Charae incorporated into the garden design.*

displays of creamy flowers. Many of the trees are labelled with their Thai names and the months in which they flower.

A damp area behind the house has been planted as a water garden with such species as *Cyperus papyrus*, *Cyperus alternifolius* (the Umbrella Plant), reedy *Typha angustifolia*, wild ferns and *Pandanus amaryllifolius*, a small variety with bright green leaves that are used in Thai cooking. Along the streams only a few ornamentals have been introduced among the native trees and shrubs already growing on the site.

Khun Charae has incorporated many of the existing trees into his garden landscape and has tried to limit introductions to those that thrive in the northern hills even though they may have been unfamiliar in the past. In doing so, he has created a garden as varied in colour and texture as it is in moods, one that lures him frequently from his busy life in Bangkok to savour its tranquil atmosphere.

A Garden by a Mountain Stream

Many housing estates have been created in the Chiang Mai area during recent years, catering mostly to Bangkok residents in search of a retreat from the capital's heat. From a horticultural standpoint, one of the most beautiful is Baan Pang Yang, created by M L Sudavadee Kriangkrai in the hills of the Samoeng District. Here the cool temperatures, especially in the winter months, and the year-round supply of water provided by a clear stream that meanders through the estate have produced gardens of exceptional vigour and also, thanks to the owner's discerning taste, notable beauty.

The dramatic floor-to-ceiling windows of the owner's bedroom offer a memorable view of soothing cascades and, on both sides of the stream, a carpet of varied colours created through masses of bright Coleus, Impatiens and various ground covers with purple, red and pale-green leaves. *Oxalis hedysaroides 'Rubra'*, a shrub from South America with rich red foliage, provides a dramatic accent here and there in the planting, which extends to the green jungle wall of towering Bananas and native plants that once covered the site.

Particularly along the stream, it is this blend of wild and introduced plants, of natural scenery and carefully landscaped areas, that gives the garden its special distinction. A huge *Cestrum nocturnum*, or Lady of the Night, spills down a hillside just as though it had always grown there. The small greenish-white flowers are inconspicuous, but in the evening it fills a nearby pavilion over the water with a powerful fragrance. Tall flowering Hedychiums, members of the Ginger family, grow freely amid the feathery fronds of local ferns and *Cyperus alternifolius*, the Umbrella Plant, forms graceful clumps beside the bubbling water.

Previous page: *A rustic bench made of old logs in the Pang Yang housing estate; behind is a stream which flows through the estate.*

Left: Hibiscus mutabilis, *among the popular names of which is the "Changeable Rose" since its large flowers change in colour from white to bright pink during the course of a single day.*

Opposite: *Mauve Bougainvillea, red and white Poinsettia and yellow* Cassia simea *display brighter colours in the cool northern hills than at lower elevations.*

Above: *Seed pods of* Bixa orellana, *the Lipstick tree; the aril surrounding the seeds inside has been used as lipstick and body paint and also as a dye for foods.*

Right: *One of the gardens in the Pang Yang estate; the yellow-flowering tree in the foreground is* Cassia siamea, *while the creeper blooming in the back is* Holmskioldia sanguinea, *the "Cup and Saucer Plant".*

Holmskioldia sanguinea, a creeper also known as the "Cup and Saucer Plant" because of the odd shape of its orange and red flowers, clambers up tree trunks as well as over gateways elsewhere in the estate.

In sunny parts of the garden, the mountain air encourages flowers of a brilliance and size that comes as a revelation to anyone who has known them only in the lowland parts of Thailand. A Lipstick tree (*Bixa orellana*) is an almost solid mass of bright red, soft-spined fruits from which a scarlet dye is extracted, and a Rose of Sharon (*Hibiscus mutabilis*) is similarly profuse with enormous, rose-like blossoms that are pure white when they open in the morning and then change slowly to deep pink by late afternoon. *Clerodendrum ugandense*, in Bangkok gardens a rather delicate sprawling shrub that flowers reluctantly, here becomes a vigorous climber with large blue flowers that resemble butterflies. Especially striking in November and December is a variety of Euphorbia which looks like a miniature Poinsettia but which in the north can become a small tree entirely covered with a snowdrift of delicate white bracts. Scarlet Salvia, also a winter specialty, creates a vivid splash of colour along the drives of the estate.

M L Sudavadee's skilled hand is evident in many of the estate's other gardens, nearly all of which display the same combination of informality, meticulous care and horticultural variety found in her own.

Above: *Along the stream grow wild Bananas as well as Cyperus alternifolius, a water-loving relative of Papyrus, popularly called the Umbrella Plant.*

Right and overleaf: *Coleus and wild ferns combine to create interesting colour and texture.*

Below: Behind M L Sudavadee's house, a slope leading to the stream is covered with a carpet of Coleus, wild ferns and Ophiopogon; most of the local trees already growing on the site were retained in this area and accentuate the natural look of the garden.

GARDENING IN THAILAND: A PERSONAL VIEW

I was around eight years old when, prompted by a sudden desire to beautify the neighbourhood, I selected several dozen rare Camellias from my grandfather's greenhouse in the American South and generously sold them up and down the street at bargain prices.

That, at least, was my story. My grandfather (and my father) took a different view. After a fearsome lecture on the evils of larceny I was forced to return to each of the houses to confess my crime and retrieve the shrub from its not always willing owner.

Thus ended my first experience with horticulture and it might well have been my last. The cultivation of ornamental plants was the least of my interests when I went off to school and remained so during the years I lived in a small New York apartment. Only when I moved to Bangkok in 1960 did I discover a passion for gardening every bit as strong as that which my grandfather had felt for his prized Camellias.

Right: *Interior garden at the Hilton, created by Sitthiporn Dhonavanik, one of Thailand's top landscape designers; Bird's Nest ferns and Spathiphyllum are among the plants that can withstand air conditioning.*

with improbably brilliant leaves, and that somewhat messy shrub called Lady of the Night (*Cestrum nocturnum*), which periodically filled the whole house with an almost overpowering perfume.

One afternoon I was walking around with the gardener and noticed that a Hibiscus was getting out of hand, putting up long unsightly branches that spoiled the shape. It was a particular favourite, with huge deep pink double flowers nearly always flowering, but I summoned up the courage to prune it back, secretly doubting whether it would ever recover.

It did, of course, with surprising speed, but that was not all. Around the time the first growth appeared, I discovered that the gardener had casually stuck all the cuttings in a patch of earth near his quarters and those, too, were growing quite luxuriantly with nothing but an occasional splash of water to encourage them.

It was a moment of Newtonian revelation. In the tropics, I suddenly perceived gardening was not the fleeting spring-and-summer endeavour it had been back home nor did it seem to require much in the way of effort or specialized skill. I quickly became reckless. I hacked back and replanted with scarcely a moment of hesitation. I

My brother thinks it was always there, a lurking genetic thing just waiting for a catalyst, and perhaps he is right; all I know is that it came upon me suddenly and quite unexpectedly.

I can even remember the precise sequence of events. My first house was a small wooden structure overlooking a shady canal that then ran along Rama IV Road, now one of Bangkok's noisier roads. It had been built by Jim Thompson of Thai silk fame, who lived there before moving to his splendid Thai-style house. He also planted the garden which, by the time I arrived, had been transformed by six rainy seasons into a lush mini-jungle of Flame trees, Hibiscus, Crinum Lilies, Crotons

tried new plants and all of them seemed to thrive. Anything, I decided, was possible, even if one didn't know the names of half the exotic vines and shrubs and ground covers available for absurdly low prices in local nurseries.

In time I learned better, often the hard way. I learned that some plants were indeed difficult, and that the quality of soil and the amount of water made a major difference. But most of all I realized that maintaining a tropical garden of pleasing design actually required more work than a similar enter-

prise conducted in temperate climates where things at least paused now and then and offered a breathing spell.

Most of these lessons I learned in my second garden which overlooked another canal, and among my teachers I was fortunate to have several of the best in Thailand.

One was the late M R Pimsai Amranand, an individual blessed with boundless energy and enthusiasm and a willingness, indeed an eagerness, to share her knowledge. Pimsai had spent most of her early life in England, and when she

Opposite top: *The author's water garden in a former house; the large leaves on the pond are those of Victoria amazonica.*

Opposite bottom: *Water Lilies and an old Thai boat outside a pavilion overlooking the pond.*

Below: *The garden of the ESCAP Conference Centre (below) is planted entirely in large containers of varying depths. Among the trees used are Ficus benjamina and Cassia surattensis, while shrubs include Pisonia, Mussaenda and golden-leafed Duranta repens; Bougainvillea is planted along the walkway between the buildings.*

Above: A waterway in the garden of the Hilton International Hotel in central Bangkok, one of the city's largest private landscapes. Variegated Pandanus, Philodendron wrightii, Fishtail ferns and variegated Alpinia grow on the far bank, while in the foreground is Thalia geniculata, a useful water plant for sunny locations.

edge about a particular species. By the time I came to know her she was already an expert and helping many others with their horticultural problems, among them (as I discovered later) Jim Thompson.

Shortly after we met I began writing a weekly gardening column in a local English-language newspaper. It appeared under the byline "Khun Suan", or "Mister Garden"—the result of a misprint of what was originally supposed to be "Khon Suan", or "Gardener". Soon I was getting a surprising volume of mail from readers who wanted to know why their Orchids refused to bloom, what to do about mealy bugs, or whether *Strelitzia reginae* could be made to bloom in Bangkok. When I couldn't think of an answer, which was often, I turned to Pimsai, who nearly always supplied it. After a couple of years, I sensibly suggested that she take over the column; she did, and in time used the material to write *Gardening in Bangkok* (1970), the first book on the subject to be published in English.

Another teacher was Princess Chumbhot of Nakhon Sawan. At her Suan Pakkad Palace she had created a unique garden: Arranged with rare plants collected from around the world and ponds that reflected the lines of traditional Thai build-

returned to her native country in the early 1950s she knew little more about the tropical side of gardening than I did on my arrival. Unlike me, however, she had acquired a wealth of practical experience in basic matters like composting, drainage and pruning, as well as a determination to translate all this into local terms. Tirelessly she combed the markets and experimented with new plants, always careful to learn their correct botanical names, and sought out gardeners who had specialized knowlings, it was justly celebrated. And at Wang Takrai, several hours' north of Bangkok, she and her husband had carved a series of even more spectacular gardens amid the jungle hills near Nakhon Nayoke. The Thai names of many ornamental trees and shrubs still include "Pantip", her first name, in recognition of the fact that they were first seen in one of her gardens.

Princess Chumbhot's renown as a hostess stemmed not only from the superb food she offered but also from the variety of her guests, most of whom shared one or another of her numerous enthusiasms. Among these were horticulture and cooking, seashells and minerals, prehistoric artefacts and modern art, skiing on both water and snow, architecture and strenuous wilderness treks. The conversation could get a bit confused at times, for example when a painter was seated next to a man who specialized in wild Gingers, but it was never dull. I fell under the horticultural category, and as such enjoyed many happy moments at her table as well as a treasured friendship that ended only with her death.

A third mentor was Thanpuying Lurasak Sampatisiri, the owner of my second house. At Nai Lert Park, the family residence next door, Thanpuying Lurasak's father had been responsible for creating a notable garden in what was in the early years of the present century a rather remote suburb, accessible only by canal. She had inherited his love for plants and his eagerness to seek out unusual ones. Together we often explored local nurseries and exchanged specimens, developing in the process a much closer relationship than is usual between landlady and tenant.

Thanks to these three teachers, I gained far more knowledge about the fundamentals of gardening in Thailand than I could ever have discovered on my own, knowledge that I have put to use in a series of houses over more than 30 years. Some of my gardens, particularly the one surrounding the house I rented from Thanpuying Lurasak on Klong Saen Sab, were large and allowed considerable creative scope; others were small and required careful plant selection; one was almost entirely occupied by a huge pond, which meant that I was exposed to what was for me a new world of aquatic plants. I do not pretend that these experiences, however varied, have raised me much above the level of enthusiastic amateur, but they have provided great pleasure and also the confidence to take on a few more professional projects.

Above: Pond at the Hilton; the large Rain tree in the background was one of the original ones on the site, planted by the owner's father some 75 years ago.

The first such project was the garden of the Hilton International Hotel, which now occupies part of the site where my second house stood. A number of prominent Thai designers worked on the hotel's extensive garden, one of the largest in Bangkok. Professor Decha Boonkham, for example, provided the basic topography and drainage system, while Khun Sitthiporn Dhonavanik created a natural-looking waterfall in one corner and an interior courtyard. None of them, however, would deny that the real credit for the landscape as it exists today belongs to Thanpuying Lurasak, who drew on her huge collection of plants and spent many weeks tramping around the muddy site deciding where they should be installed.

I served as her assistant and, in the process, developed a working method that I have used in every job since. This is almost the opposite of the method used by most professional landscape designers, in which detailed scale drawings showing every single component down to the last small pot of ground cover are prepared far in advance. While admiring the orderliness of this approach and accepting that on many projects it is necessary for arriving at a budget, I find it almost impossible to emu-

late. I can provide a list of the types of plants I want to use and even an approximate number; but when it comes to the installation I need to have the actual building(s) more or less completed so that I have a clear idea of sight lines, areas of shadow and sun, wind patterns and, rather more vague, the general atmosphere.

Fortunately for me, another friend, the architect M L Tri Devakul, is sympathetic to this method and I have been able to work on a number of his projects. One was the Australian Embassy, built largely around and over a series of ponds; the lush, jungle-type garden was designed by Bruce Mackenzie, a fervent proponent of natural landscapes. I acted as the local consultant advising on plant material and overseeing installation when he could not be present. Several huge Rain trees grew on the site, and a major concern was their preservation. Then as now, it was the custom of builders in Thailand to simply cut down any trees that might impede construction, arguing (with the same logic that spurred my early gardening efforts) that others would grow quickly. These, however, were perhaps 50 years old, and they constituted a major part of the compound's charm; indeed, the buildings had been designed

with them as central features. In the end, they survived, partly through vigilance, but mostly because of a penalty clause in the building contract—and I gained valuable experience working with a designer whose love of plants was contagious.

Other projects have included hotel and private gardens in the island of Phuket, where exposure to monsoon winds from the sea has presented very different challenges; a conference centre in Bangkok where most of the garden consisted of large planter-boxes of varying depths and where drainage and soil quality were of paramount importance; and a garden in Chiang Mai that proved susceptible to annual floods and had to be planted (or, rather, replanted) accordingly.

My gardening years in Thailand have been happy ones, and when I look back on them it is always with a sense of wonder at the distance I have travelled from my grandfather's greenhouse. At the same time, each new garden I plant, whether it be my own or someone else's, brings a fresh awareness of how much there is still to learn.

Opposite: The author's present garden; Spathiphyllum are used as a ground cover beneath an old Cordia which has grown into a small tree. The terracotta pot is from a Thai kiln.

IDEAS FOR SMALL GARDENS

Perhaps the most significant change in Thai gardens over the past decade or so is that most have become increasingly smaller. As recently as the early 1970s even a modest Bangkok compound offered a substantial amount of planting space and grander ones had room for mini-parks with lakes and impressive trees that spread shady canopies over large areas. Today, as a rule, only resorts and a few country estates enjoy such horticultural freedom. The average gardener, not just in the capital but also in many provincial cities, is forced to work in a relatively confined space, often surrounded by neighbouring high-rises and inspired as much by the need to screen for privacy as by the desire for a varied landscape.

Some plant-lovers, however, approach this as a challenge rather than as a hardship. Local nurseries offer numerous smaller trees to replace the spreading giants that characterized older compounds, along with an increasingly large selection of ornamental shrubs and ground covers, while a sense of surprise and discovery can be achieved through a few dramatic plantings and unusual pathways, and architecture can be utilized to integrate house and garden. There are even advantages to gardening on such a limited scale: many potted specimens can be used and thus moved about for varied effects and, important to busy city dwellers, far less physical labour is required for the non-stop duties imposed by the tropics.

With determination and perhaps a few ideas adapted from the gardens shown here, even the tiniest spaces can be given a sense of distinction and satisfy a craving for restful green.

Opposite: *Potted* Catharanthus rosea *bring a spot of colour to this shady pool in the city garden of Khun Sunanta Tulyadhan; the tree on the left is* Brassia actinophylla, *popularly called the Octopus tree, while large leaves on the right are those of a Philodendron. The use of stones and pebbles around the pond create such a natural atmosphere that one would never know that the garden is in the heart of metropolitan Bangkok.*

A narrow strip of land along the edge of a parking lot outside the Bensley Design Group Studio has been transformed into a varied mini-garden. Laterite stone gives an interesting texture to the wall, while a contemporary terracotta bas-relief made in northern Thailand provides a decorative focal point. Tall, purple-stemmed Alocasias (Elephant's Ears) are used for height at the back, together with such coloured-foliage plants as variegated Dracaena, Cordyline and dwarf *Pandanus pygmaeus*. In a semi-public place, all have the added advantage of being low-maintenance plants, requiring only occasional watering and trimming of dead leaves.

Even a blank wall can be turned into an outdoor art exhibit, as Pittaya Bunnag has done with one along a tiled courtyard in his Chiang Mai house. Antique plates from his large collection are arranged in a group just below a night lamp, as well as an old lintel from a northern Thai house. Other features that enhance the area include a weathered tree trunk used as a stand for a pot of ferns, a Thai-style cabinet, panelling to disguise an otherwise mundane gate and wooden roof shingles on an overhang.

Though part of a large family compound, the garden of Sittichai and Tida Tanpipat has relatively limited space and privacy has been achieved through a few existing trees and dense planting, together with strategically placed potted specimens. Typical is this arrangement near the entrance, in which ferns, flowering Bananas and a small-leafed Ficus are used as a lush setting for some stone figures brought back from a visit to Bali. Adorning the large statue of a Hindu goddess is a typically Balinese wreath of marigolds, while below are two elephants mounted on laterite blocks.

Sculpture can be a dramatic focal point in a garden. Here a Balinese image of Ganesha, elephant-headed son of Siva and Parbati and regarded as the god of knowledge or arts, is prominately displayed on a base of laterite blocks just outside the front terrace of the Tanpipat house. Among the potted plants that surround it are giant Maidenhair fern and Bird's Nest fern (*Asplenium nidus*). The old water jar below is Thai. The statue is adorned daily with blossoms such as Hibiscus and Plumeria for added visual appeal.

Close neighbours, a low wall and a very narrow strip of garden space were some of the problems confronted by Brian Sherman, a partner in the Bensley Design Group, and his wife Kelly. Instant screening was provided by a length of split-bamboo fencing, easily assembled from local materials, assisted after a short time by planting. The most effective specimens are two Traveller's palms (*Ravenala madagascariensis*), fast-growing members of the Banana family with huge, paddle-shaped leaves, between which an old earthenware water jar is displayed on a laterite base. Other plants to offer varied textures and colour include Codiaeum, Heliconias, Spathiphyllum and *Dracaena marginata* (the Rainbow Plant).

How can a carport be made interesting? This is a question often asked, often left unresolved by even the keenest garden-lover, no doubt on the grounds that only the most alert guest is likely to notice it. Sittichai and Tida Tantipat would not agree. Determined to bring greenery into every part of their compound, they have turned one side into a sitting area with an old marble-topped table, local terracotta jars and a wide variety of large, potted plants. The same sort of arrangement was continued across the drive near the entrance to the house, with a tall Dracaena, a large Fishtail fern and a Ficus trained as a standard.

Lacking the space for permanent plants in the ground, the small courtyard just inside the gate of Bill Bensley's Bangkok house has been turned into a luxuriant garden of potted specimens collected by his partner Jirachai Rengthong, accented with decorative objects. The arrangement shown on the right here is composed mostly of Cordylines, Dieffenbachias and Aglaonemas, set on laterite blocks to form a dramatic pyramid of different leaf colours and shapes, while on the left, above the large leaves of a Monstera is a blue-and-white kiln waster with an arresting shape. The paving of irregular cement bricks also gives distinction to the area.

Privacy became a major concern to Inge and Tanu Malakul when their house in one of Bangkok's most popular residential areas was gradually surrounded by high-rise condominiums. Unwilling to give up the pleasures of outdoor living, they created a lath-covered deck off their living room, disguised the walls with wooden trellises and filled the area with some of Inge's large collection of ornamental plants. Among the specimens overlooked by a ceramic Chinese goddess are a giant Spathiphyllum, Calathea, Maranta and white-veined *Anthurium cristillanum*; more sunlight behind is adequate for a pot of feathery Bamboo.

At least half a day's sunlight is necessary for the healthy growth of most water plants in an open jar. Lotus and water lilies require soil, either in the jar itself or in a sunken pot, but other specimens will float decoratively on the surface like the Water Lettuce (*Pistia stratiotes*) shown here. Others worth trying include Water Poppy (*Hydrocleys nymphoides*), with bright yellow flowers; white Water Snowflake (*Nymphoides indica*); and even the much-reviled Water Hyacinth (*Eichornia crassipes*), which can be kept under control in such a limited space.

Thai gardeners are fortunate enough to have a large selection of inexpensive, locally produced water jars, almost any of which can be used as a striking garden ornament. Shown here is one of the many glazed examples available in Thai plant markets, with a ceramic frog added for an extra note of interest; Hibiscus and Plumeria blossoms float on the surface.

Flowers floating in a water jar brighten up a terrace or garden for a party. The combination on the right is different varieties of Hibiscus and Plumeria, while below yellow Chrysanthemums provide a bright colour accent. However, almost any readily available blossom can be used, either collected in the garden or bought from a flower shop. Except for Orchids, most tropical flowers do not last very long when floated in this way, so they should be cut as near to the time of use as possible.

Attention to detail can make all the difference in a really small garden space, like this area just inside the entrance to the compound of Marisa Viravaidya and Douglas Clayton in Bangkok. An unusual pattern of bricks draws attention to a terracotta lamp from Bali in the centre, while an unattractive cement wall behind the spirit house has been covered with split Bamboo (treated to protect it from termites and other pests) and a large jar is planted with Water Lilies. A jungle-like atmosphere is created through plants with ornamental foliage and creepers like the Philodendron on the right.

In the same garden shown above, a brick pathway in a herringbone pattern leads to one of several Thai-style houses in the compound. Though the total planted area is small, a sense of variety is achieved through the creation of several areas, each with its own focal point. Contributing to the tropical effect in this one are a tall stand of Golden Bamboo, Dieffenbachia with fancy leaves and a Honeysuckle vine that clambers up a trellis to the balcony of the house and periodically fills the area with its fragrant flowers. The Balinese ornaments are illuminated at night.

The Tantipat garden feels much larger than it actually is due to a number of interesting areas separated from one another by dense plantings. Here under the spreading branches of a large fragrant white Plumeria a space has been set aside for an old marble-topped table and two chairs. A Ficus tree, Rhapis palms and a fan palm provide a soothing green background, while on the left is an antique water jar which has a rustic brown glaze.

Bill Bensley, who has been responsible for many major garden designs in Thailand, Indonesia and Hawaii, has a far smaller scale on which to work at his own home in Bangkok. Here, too, though, his inventive skills at creating distinctive atmospheres are evident as in this tiny space off his lower terrace. A "lawn" of tufted, grass-like *Ophiopogon japonicus* surrounds a square of concrete blocks set into the ground and a contemporary reproduction of the head of a Khmer ruler serves as a decorative feature. The trunks of tall Royal palms lend a formal touch to the tropical mass behind.

Laterite blocks, which can be found in many shapes, make an attractive, natural-looking pathway, especially in a sunny area where they are less likely to become slippery during the rainy season. In the example shown here they have been set flush with the grass and spaced for easy walking. Garden lamps have been fashioned from old tree trunks while large jars with Lilies and other water plants add interest along the way.

Granite slabs set into the lawn make an informal pathway through this garden, past beds densely planted with Heliconias, Crinum Lilies, palms and Spider Lilies (*Hymenocallis littoralis*). Though the pattern may seen random, it is in fact carefully planned for ease of walking and the stones set deep to allow the grass to be cut by machine. At the far end, taller plants form a natural entryway into yet another part of the landscape.

BIBLIOGRAPHY

Amranand, Pimsai, *Gardening in Bangkok* (The Siam Society, Bangkok, 1970)

Amranand, Pimsai and Warren, William, *Gardening in Bangkok* (Revised Edition) (The Siam Society, Bangkok, 1994)

Bar-Zvi, David, *Tropical Gardening* (Pantheon Books, New York, 1996)

Berry, Fred and Kress, W. John, *Heliconia, An Identification Guide*, (Smithsonian Institution Press, Washington, 1991)

Bown, Deni, *Aroids: Plants of the Arum Family* (Century Hutchinson, Ltd., London,1988)

Brown, R. Frank, *The Cordyline* (Valkaria Tropical Garden, Florida, 1994)

Bruggeman, L., *Tropical Plants and their Cultivation* (Thames and Hudson, London, 1957)

Clay, Horace F. and Hubbard, James C., *The Hawai'i Garden: Tropical Exotics* (University Press of Hawaii, Honolulu, 1977)

Gilliland, H.B., *Common Malayan Plants* (University of Malaya Press, Kuala Lumpur, 1958)

Graf, Alfred Byrd, *Tropica: Color Cyclopedia of Exotic Plants and Trees* (Roehrs Company, New Jersey, USA, 1981)

Greensill, T.M., *Gardening in the Tropics* (Evans Brothers Ltd., London, 1964)

Holttum, R.E. and Enoch, Ivan, *Gardening in the Tropics* (Times Editions Pte Ltd, Singapore, 1991)

Kuck, Loraine E. and Tongg, Richard C., *Hawaiian Flowers and Flowering Trees* (Charles E. Tuttle Co., Tokyo, 1960)

Lotschert, W. and Beese, G., *Tropical Plants* (William Collins Sons & Co., Ltd, London, 1983)

McMakin, Patrick D., *A Field Guide to the Flowering Plants of Thailand* (White Lotus Co., Ltd., Bangkok, 1988)

Macmillan, H.F., *Tropical Planting and Gardening* (Macmillan and Company, London, 1935)

Menninger, Edwin A., *Flowering Trees of the World* (Hearthside Press, Inc, New York, 1962)

Merrill, Elmer D., *Plant Life of the Pacific World* (Charles E. Tuttle Co., Tokyo, 1981)

Polunin, Ivan, *Plants and Flowers of Singapore* (Times Editions Pte Ltd., Singapore, 1987)

Smitinand, Tem, *Thai Plant Names* (Royal Forest Department, Bangkok, 1980)

Steiner, Dr. Mona Lisa, *Philippine Ornamental Plants* (Enrian Press, Manila, 3rd ed 1986)

Thomas, Arthur, *Gardening in Hot Countries* (Faber & Faber, London, 1965)

Warren, William, *The Tropical Garden* (Thames and Hudson, London, 1991)

INDEX

Acorus gramineus　32, 90
Acoelorrhaphe wrightii 'silver saw'　51
Acrostichum aureum　75, 79
Acalypha　126, 155
Acalypha wilkesiana　115, 121, 154
Aechmea group　56
African Oil palm　76, 79
African Tulip tree　124, 133, 151
Agave　102
Agave angustifolia　117
Agave americana　109, 159
Aglaonema　18, 19, 31, 38, 40, 41, 93, 145, 183
Aglaonema pictum　46
Allamanda　55, 61, 76, 82, 135
Alocasia　29, 32, 45, 82, 93, 180
Alocasia macrorrhizos　124
Alpinia　19, 31, 32, 135, 141
Alpinia purpurata　29, 32, 34, 93, 129, 136
Alpinia zerumbet　34
Amherstia nobilis　145
Andaman Sea　58, 90, 97
Anthurium　53
Anthurium cristallinum　183
Arecastrum romanzoffianum　52
Artabotrys hexapetalus　20, 76
Ascocentrum　108
Asplenium　93
Asplenium nidus　46, 95, 126, 138, 181
Association of Siamese Architects　86
Avocado Pear　144, 145
Ayutthaya　11, 16, 22
Baan Pang Yang　162, 164
Baan Rim Thai Sai Thorn　149
Baan Soi Klang　45
Bali　124, 152, 180
Bamboo　41, 115, 116, 135, 141
Bambusa ventricosa　147
Banana　19, 32, 37, 126, 166
Bangkok　22, 24, 45, 47, 56, 58, 70, 102, 106, 178
Barlaria cristata　158
Barringtonia asiatica　45, 47, 61, 86, 93, 99

Bauhinia　115
Bauhinia acuminata　64
Beaucarnea recurvata　112
Beaumontia grandiflora　76
Bensley Design Group　31, 75, 124, 182
Betel Nut palm　11, 22, 138
Bird of Paradise　76
Bird's Nest fern　46, 93, 95, 126, 138, 170, 181
Bismarckia nobilis　51, 54, 75
Bixa orellana　164, 165
Bodhi tree　13
Bombax ceiba　19
Bonsai　14
Borassodendron　56
Bottlebrush　41, 76
Bougainvillea　18, 19, 41, 47, 61, 64, 66, 68, 70, 72, 76, 86, 93, 99, 100, 101, 102, 107, 115, 118, 120, 145, 147, 164, 173
Brassaia　47
Brassaia actinophylla　47, 76, 178
Brassiolaeliocattleya 'Alma Kee'　109
Brassiolaeliocattleya 'Lucky Strike'　109
Bromeliad　56
Brunfelsia pauciflora 'floribunda compacta' (eximia)　152
Buddha's Belly Bamboo　147
Burma　102, 145
Butea monosperma　47
Butia capita　52
Cabbage　149, 150
Caesalpinia　32
Caladium　18
Calathea　32, 47, 145, 182
Calliandra　141, 155
Calliandra surinamensis　158
Callistemon lanceolatus　41, 76
Calotropis gigantea　86
Camellia　170
Cananga odorata　20
Canna　64, 72, 107
Carissa macrocarpa 'Humphreyi Variegata'　154
Carnation　12, 149, 158, 159

Caryota mitis　41, 76
Cassia bakeriana　152, 153
Cassia fistula　20, 68
Cassia siamea　118, 119, 120, 164
Cassia surattensis　41, 173
Casuarina　62
Casuarina equisetifolia　93
Catharanthus rosea　178
Catteleya 'Queen Sirikit'　109
Celosia　126
Century Plant　117
Cestrum nocturnum　162, 172
Champaca　20
Champi　17
Chandhana　17
"Changeable Rose"　164
Chao Phraya River　22, 24, 141
Chiang Mai　68, 102, 106, 109, 112, 124, 128, 138, 147, 149, 162
Chiang Rai　107
Chiva-Som Health Spa　58, 64
Chula Chakrabongse, Prince　17, 58, 60
Chumbhot, Princess　175
Chrysalidocarpus palm　41
Chrysanthemum　107, 185
Citrus medica　144
Cleome　112, 118, 158, 159
Clerodendrum fragrans　19
Clerodendrum quadriloculare　158
Clerodendrum ugandense　165
Clusia　144
"Coco-de-Mer"　52
Coconut palm　22, 58, 60, 62, 64, 75, 76, 82, 84, 86
Codiaeum　18, 19, 29, 31, 32, 76, 93, 135, 145, 147, 182
Coleus　107, 147, 162, 166, 167
Congea tomentosa　145, 152
Coniferae　115, 158
Copernicia baileyana　51
Copernicia macroglossa　51
Copperpod　82
Coral tree　144, 151
Cordia　177
Cordyline　19, 27, 29, 31, 32, 34, 47, 76, 143, 180, 183

Cork tree　151
Corypha　55
Corypha elata　51
Costus speciosus　93
Crateva adansonii　79
Crateva religiosa　76
Crepe Ginger　93
Crinum　32, 34, 42, 58, 61, 77, 126, 127, 151, 172, 188
Crinum amabile　129
Crinum asiaticum　68, 93, 126
Crotons　19, 172
Crown Flower　86
"Cuban Petticoat Palm"　51
"Cup and Saucer Plant"　165
Cuphea　34
Cuphea miniata　114
Cupressus　102
Cupressus sempervirens　112, 118, 119, 121, 158
Cycad　52, 107
Cycadaceae family　52
Cycas　55, 86, 112, 118
Cycas circinalis　52
Cymbopogon citratus　149, 150
Cyperus alternifolius　38, 41, 75, 161, 162, 166
Cyperus papyrus　161
Dahlia　107
Daisy　12, 107, 159
Damrong Rachanuphab, Prince　13
Dasylirion　52
Dasylirion glaucophyllum　52
Date palm　76
Delonix regia　27, 68, 126, 133
Dendrobium　109
Dendrobium fredrichsiana　108
Dendrobium lindleyi　108
Dendrobium 'Mme Pompadour'　109
Dhonavan, Sitthiporn　38, 170
Dianella ensifolia　48, 124
Dictyosperma album　52
Dieffenbachia　18, 19, 32, 34, 40, 41, 45, 46, 47, 76, 77, 93, 183, 186
Dimocarpus longan　133
Diospyros rhodocalyx　14, 70, 72
Double Coconut　52

Dracaena   17, 64, 76, 180, 182
Dracaena fragrans   41, 45, 126
Dracaena loureiri   116
Dracaena marginata   182
Draecaena reflexa   149, 151
Duranta repens   32, 68, 107, 115, 116, 120, 121, 129, 158, 173
Durian   11
Dusit Rayavadee Resort   84, 87
Dwarf fan palm   51
Dwarf Tamarind tree   17
Egyptian Papyrus   151
Eichornia crassipes   184
Elaeis guineensis   76, 79
Elaeocarpus hygrophilus Kurtz   141
Elephant's Ear   29, 32, 45, 82, 93, 124, 180
Eranthemum pulchellum   76
Erythrina   133
Erythrina fusca   144
Erythrina variegata   135, 151
Etlingera elatior   45, 47, 126, 152, 153
Eucalyptus   79
Euphorbia   107, 165
Euphorbia pulcherrima   116, 147
Fern   19, 38, 41, 90, 114, 141, 161, 166, 180, 181
Ficus   31, 41, 46, 47, 48, 68, 96, 115, 121, 129, 133, 158, 161, 180, 182, 187
Ficus benjamina   47, 173
Ficus elastica   29, 47
Ficus religiosa   13
"Fire Bush"   154
Fishtail fern   182
Fishtail palm   41, 76
Flame tree   27, 68, 72, 133, 172
Flame of the Forest   47
Four Aces Consultants Co Ltd   84
Galphimia glauca   152
Gardenia   12, 64, 145
Gardenia jasminoides   144, 152
Gerbera   19
Gervaise, Nicholas   8
Giant Mangrove fern   75, 79
Gliricidia sepium   151

Golden Bamboo   29, 32, 126, 127, 186
Golden Bells   149, 151, 158
Golden Crinum   76
Golden Dewdrop   32
Golden Duranta   77, 115, 155
Golden Shower tree   20, 68
Golden Tea   116
Grand Palace, Bangkok   13, 14, 16, 17, 22
Gulf of Thailand   24, 58, 64, 68
Gustavia superba   144
Had Nopparat Thara National Park   86
Hamelia patens   68, 154
Hedychium   162
Hedychium coronarium   147
Heliconia   19, 29, 41, 47, 52, 86, 87, 107, 126, 128, 133, 135, 141, 151, 182, 188
Heliconia caribaea   135
Heliconia caribaea Lamarck   129
Heliconia chartacea   141
Heliconia indica   32, 90, 124
Heliconia orthotricha cv. 'Total Eclipse'   131
Heliconia pendula   68
Heliconia psittacorum   68, 135
Heliconia psittacorum cv. 'St. Vincent Red'   131
Heliconia psittacorum cv. 'Lady Di'   68
Heliconia stricta cv. 'Firebird'   130
Heliconia x nickeriensis Maas & de Rooy   151
Hibiscus   19, 32, 47, 64, 66, 76, 77, 86, 143, 145, 158, 172, 184, 185
Hibiscus tiliaceus   86, 93
Hibiscus mutabilis   164, 165
Hilton Hotel, Bangkok   170, 174, 175, 177
Honeysuckle   186
Holmskioldia sanguinea   165
Hoya   53
Hua Hin   60, 64, 70, 72, 75, 112
Hydrocleys nymphoides   77, 152, 184
Hymenocallis   64

Hymenocallis littoralis   90, 99, 100, 126, 188
Hyophorbe vershaffeltii   55
Impatiens   107, 114, 162
Imperial Palace, Beijing   17
Indian Cork tree   124
Indian Laburnum   20
Indian Ocean   58
Ixora   29, 32, 34, 68, 72, 76, 107, 154
Ixora javanica   129
Jade Vine   107, 137
Jasmine   12, 17
Jasminium rex   20, 141
Jasminium sambac   17
Juniperus   155, 158
Justicia   76, 77, 90
Justicia fragilis   90, 147
Kaffir Lime   18
Kata Beach   62
Ked   17
Kerriodoxa elegans   52
Khao mor   14, 17
Khao Wang   18
Khoi   14
Kigelia pinnata   145
Klai Kangvol   70
Krabi   84
Lady of the Night   162, 172
Lagerstroemia   68
Lagerstroemia speciosa   158
Lamduan   17
Lamyai   133
Lanna Kingdom   102
Lanna Resort   112, 115, 119, 120
Lantana   19, 151
Lan-tom   18
Laos   102
Latania loddegesii   76
Lemon Grass   149, 150, 152
Lipstick tree   164, 165
Livistona fan palm   22, 41, 51
Livistona decipiens   51
Livistona muelleri   51
Lodoicea maldivica   52
Longan   133
Lotus   11, 13, 64, 151

Loubère, Simon de la   12
Lumchiek   17
Ma-fuang   18
Ma-kham   14
Ma-kok nam   141
Ma-krut   18
Ma-la-kaw   18
Ma-muang   18
Ma-yom   18
Mae Rim District   124
Mae Sa Valley   106, 112
Magnolia   17
Mai dat   13, 14, 17
Maidenhair fern   181
Mali-sorn   17
Malpighia coccigera   47, 68
Mammea siamensis   17
Mango   11, 18, 45, 64
Maranta   41, 47, 145
Marigold   118, 121
Mekong River   135
Melia azedarach   41, 151
Melodorum fruticosum   17
Michelia champaca alba   17, 20
Millingtonia   126, 149
Millingtonia hortensis   124, 151
Mimusops elengi   17
Mock Orange   32, 151
Mok   14
Mongkut, King   17
Monstera   183
Mucuna bennettii   132, 141, 144
Muntabhorn, Pusadee   41
Murraya paniculata   32, 68, 76, 151
Musa coccinea   136
Mussaenda   60, 107, 145, 173
Myriophyllum aquaticum   153
Nelumbo nucifera   11, 13
Nai Harn Beach   61
Nang yaem   19
Narai, King   11
Nelumbo nucifera   64
New Guinea Creeper   107, 132, 141, 144
Ngiu   19
Nymphaea   75, 126
Nymphoides indica   184

Octopus tree 47, 178
Ophiopogon 32, 147, 167
Ophiopogon japonicus 158, 187
Orchids 19, 53, 108, 109, 141
Oxalis hedysaroides 'Rubra' 162
Palmae family 51
Pandanus 41, 77, 86, 93, 97, 101
Pandanus amaryllifolius 34, 151, 161
Pandanus odoratissimus 17, 61
Pandanus pygmaeus 68, 180
Pandanus veitchii 42, 48
Papaya 18
Papyrus 161, 166
Pattaya 60, 70, 112
Peacock flower 32
Peltophorum pterocarpum 68, 76, 82
Persea americana 144
Persian Lilac 41, 151
Petchaburi 13
Petunia 149
Philodendron 32, 34, 46, 47, 52, 90, 95, 178, 186
Philodendron wrightii 32, 41, 45, 47
Phlox 158
Phoenix dactylifera 76, 82
Phoenix palm 112, 151
Phra Nang 84, 88
Phuket 60
Phuket Yacht Club 60, 61
Phyllanthus acidus 18, 20
Phyllanthus myrtifolius 114, 158
Pikul 17
Pilea 143
Pilea cardieri 114
Pimsai Amranand, M R 19, 173
Pineapple 58
Ping River 106, 128, 143
Pink Shower tree 152, 153
Pink Trumpet tree 133
Pisonia 60, 61, 64, 173
Pisonia alba 47
Pistia stratiotes 79, 184
Pithecellobium dulce 137
Platycerium coronarium 95, 126
Plumeria 12, 18, 19, 47, 68, 72, 76, 126, 128, 133, 147, 184, 185, 187

Plumeria rubra 20
Poinsettia 145, 147, 164, 165
Polyalthia longifolia pendula 90, 93
Polyscias 76
Pong Yang Garden Village 102, 112, 114, 115, 116, 118
"Pony-tail Palm" 112
Potato tree 144, 145, 158
Premier Group 84
Prichardia 51
Prichardia pacifica 76
Pride of India 158
Prong 19, 86
Pseudocalymona alliaceum x mussaenda 107
Ptychosperma macarthurii 51
Quisqualis indica 76
Railway Hotel, Hua Hin 70
Rain tree 27, 29, 31, 72, 133, 177
Rainbow Plant 182
Rama II, King 17
Rama IV, King 18
Rama VI, King 60
Rangoon Creeper 76
Ravenala madagascariensis 76, 182
Red Ginger 29, 32, 34, 42, 93, 129, 136
Regent hotel, Bangkok 38
Regent hotel, Chiang Mai 124
Reisinger, Reimund 31
Rhapis palm 27, 41, 47, 107, 187
Rhoeo 40
Rhoeo discolor 124
Rhopaloblaste 51
Rhynchostylus 109
Rhynchostylis gigantea 54
Rose 12, 107, 147
Rose of Sharon 165
Roystonea regia 47, 68
Royal Garden Village 75, 76, 82
Royal palm 47, 68
Rubber plant 29
Rubber tree 58
Sabal palm 51
Salvia 107, 118, 121, 126, 158, 159, 165
Samanea saman 27, 133

Samoeng District 162
Sampatisiri, Thanpuying Lurasak 175
Sanchezia nobilis 158
Sansevieria 124, 126
Sansevieria trifasciata 17
Saraca 12
Sarapee 17
Sausage tree 145
Scaevola 84, 86, 93
Scaevola taccada 61
Scindapsus 32, 41, 77
Sea Almond 93, 98, 99
Sea Hibiscus 86, 93
Sea Lettuce 61, 86, 93
Sea Oak 93
Seashore Screwpine 61, 86, 93, 101
Sheraton Grande Laguna, Phuket 62
Siam Mariposa 128
Siamese Rough Bush 14, 70, 72
Singapore Holly 68
Soi Klang 45
Solanum bipinartifidum 144, 145, 147, 158
Song of India 149, 151
Spathiphyllum 27, 32, 34, 40, 41, 42, 47, 64, 126, 170, 177, 182
Spathodea campanulata 76, 124, 126, 133 151
Spider Lily 99, 126, 188
Stag's Horn fern 95, 126
Star Gooseberry 16, 20
Starfruit 18
Streblus asper 14, 47
Strelitziaceae 76
Strelitzia reginae 174
Strongylodon macrobotrys 137
Suan 19
Sukothai 8, 13
Sukhumwit Road 45
Sunthorn Phu 17
Syngonium 42
Tabebuia 68, 76
Tabebuia rosea 133
Tabernaemontana 64
Tako 14, 72

Tamarind 14, 17
Teak 102, 147
Tectona grandis 102
Tecoma stans 149, 151, 158
Terminalia catappa 61, 93, 98, 101
Thalia geniculata 38, 75, 79, 126, 151, 152
Thevetia 76
Thompson, Jim 22, 27, 29, 31, 32, 34, 37
Thompson, P A 12
Thuja orientalis 118, 155, 158
Thunbergia erecta 158
Thunbergia grandiflora 32
Tiger's Claw 133
Torch Ginger 45, 47, 126, 152, 153
Traveller's palm 76, 82, 182
Tuberose 12
Typha angustifolia 48, 75, 126, 151, 161
Umbrella plant 38, 161, 162, 166
Vanda 108
Vanda coerulea 108
Victoria amazonica 173
Wat Mongkut, Bangkok 11
Wat Po 13
Wat Raj Bophit 13
Water Canna 38, 126, 151
Water Hyacinth 184
Water Lettuce 79, 184
Water Lily 47, 75, 77, 79, 152, 173
Water Poppy 77, 152, 184
Water Snowflake 184
Wedelia triloba 58, 60, 66, 68
"Weeping Cabbage" 51
White Ginger 147
Wodyetia palm 'foxtail' 51
Wrightia religiosa 14, 41, 64, 76, 158
Yellow Flame tree 76, 82
Yesterday-Today-and-Tomorrow Plant 152
Zamia furfuracea 52
Zinnia 126